SO BE IT

O R

THE CHIPS ARE DOWN

SO BE IT

OR THE CHIPS ARE DOWN

[AINSI SOIT-IL, OU LES JEUX SONT FAITS]

ANDRÉ GIDE

TRANSLATED FROM THE FRENCH,

WITH AN INTRODUCTION AND NOTES, BY

Justin O'Brien

1960
CHATTO & WINDUS
LONDON

Published by
Chatto and Windus Ltd
London

PRINTED BY THE REPLIKA PROCESS
IN GREAT BRITAIN BY
LUND HUMPHRIES
LONDON · BRADFORD

FOR MY DAUGHTER

Catherine Jean Lambert

INTRODUCTION
BY
JUSTIN O'BRIEN

In late 1947, about the time he received the
Nobel Prize, André Gide noted in his *Journals:* "I
shall be able to say: 'So be it' to whatever happens
to me, were it even ceasing to exist, disappearing
after having been." Indeed, the serenity of his last
years found its perfect expression in the oft-
repeated words *Ainsi soit-il* which he was to use as
the title for his final manuscript.

But, despite his resignation to the inevitable,
there was one thing Gide could not forgo even on
the threshold of death: the inveterate habit of
probing into himself and setting down his impressions. The very last page he wrote, six days before
his death, forms a most revealing confession in this
regard. Although still quite recognizably his, the
hand is shaky at first, becoming firmer as it continues. In the first two or three lines, certain
words, through the repetition of a syllable, seem to
stammer; but visibly the mind clears as the hand
gains in suppleness. There is something infinitely

pathetic in the observation that the old man, at the end of a literary career extending over more than sixty years, is tormented, between two periods of coma, by the thought that he may not have said all he had it in him to say, that he may want to add something, he knows not what. And, sure enough, after letting his pen run on for a few minutes, he does succeed in recording as his *novissima verba*, before again sinking into unconsciousness, a beautiful ambiguous sentence, stylistically perfect like the best of his prose.

The whole of this ultimate work from the hand of Gide is motivated by the same desire to leave nothing essential unsaid. In mid-1949, shortly before his eightieth birthday, he had deliberately closed up his vast *Journals,* begun before the age of twenty. But soon he must have missed the pleasure of setting down his daily reflections in a little notebook, for by the following summer—despite the absorbing work of polishing his own theatrical adaptation of an early novel, despite the organization of various voluminous collections of his correspondence, despite the declarations he was constantly called upon to write for different groups from Venice to Tokyo—he had begun this manuscript.

When I saw Gide again in the last two months of his life, after a year's interruption in our conversations, he spoke at length of this work, frequently opening the fat folder on his table to show a page or two. Refusing to consider those pages as related to his *Journals,* he insisted rather on their difference from everything he had ever written and likened them more than once to the *Essays* of Montaigne. Their originality for him lay in their rapid, spontaneous composition, without retouching or even rereading. He admitted that he had often striven for such a free-and-easy manner in the *Journals,* as a protest against his innate concern for form, but each time he had soon given up. "This time," he said, "I am going through with it to the very end." It was impossible to tell whether he meant the end of the manuscript or the end of his life. Probably he thought of the two as synchronous.

But he did not, for all his eighty-one years, necessarily think of them as imminent. Having become attached, for instance, to the American fountain pen and its special ink that I had given him thirteen months earlier, he found in late January 1951 that he was on the point of running out of the ink, which was not then available in Paris. Through friends I found him a fresh bottle, which he planned to take to Marrakech with him. Only his fatal illness a fortnight later cancelled the trip and put an abrupt end to his manuscript.

The unpremeditated manner of writing naturally gives this work a conversational flavour—that is, the flavour of André Gide's conversation, of which his close friend Roger Martin du Gard noted:

Gide seems to be continually playing hide-and-seek with himself, and with his interlocutor. His conversation—broken into by parentheses, reminiscences, anecdotes, and bursts of delicious fooling—has the gratuitousness, the unconcern, of a game; it is full of turns and returns, details touched and retouched, pauses and hesitations, brusque advances and brusque retreats; it is a mixture of modesty and cynicism, reticence and candour, unexpected avowals and the discreetest of allusions. Sometimes as plain as a straight line, sometimes as baffling as the convolutions of a maze, it makes its way—regretfully, one might suppose—toward its final precision. That it is always aiming at this precision is clear: but it never seems in any hurry to get to it, so great is its pleasure in the long

*twilit pauses, which culminate in that blazing mo-
ment when the whole question is resolved in a few
astonishing phrases. But whether these phrases are
the result of some lightning flash of happy in-
spiration or of an opportune verbal accident, or
whether they are the fruit of experience, the out-
come of lengthy meditation—all this one cannot
say.*[1]

As Gide was well aware in writing *So Be It*,
the inevitable hazard of such a carefree form,
which aims not to "sort out the spontaneous run
of the mill," is repetition. Hence we are not surprised to find here certain incidents and reflections
that he had recorded years before in his *Journals*.
Beside them, however, as the octogenarian's mind
ranged over the fullness of his past, stand pages
containing revelations even for readers most familiar with André Gide and his work. In a voluminous
and exhaustive study of the writer's youth, for instance, Dr. Jean Delay cites a passage from *So Be
It* as the most revealing of Gide's many confessions.
He refers to the page in which Gide tells how the
image of his mother and that of his wife fuse in

[1] *Recollections of André Gide*, translated by John Russell
(New York: Viking Press; 1953), pp. 118–19.

his dreams into a single person playing an inhibitory role. Other numerous comments here about his sexual preferences—even though they come after so many calculated indiscretions—are equally valuable for an understanding of his psychology.

Whether he is discussing such matters, indulging in futile regrets, analyzing his untrustworthy memory or his strange disbelief in reality, developing his thoughts about Molière or social injustice or the art of acting, or simply adding to his recollections of his travels in the U.S.S.R. and in the Congo, Gide continues here his lifelong work of destroying the legends that had grown up about him and presenting himself as he really was—or at least as he saw himself. In order to complete the image he had already built up in his many works, he had at the end of his life to show us the effects of age, the physical infirmities, the doubts and hesitations, the waning appetite for life. And to his credit it must be said that such lucid admissions are almost without precedent in literature. As he notes here, "I had not made arrangements to live so old"; but, having lived on, he quite naturally took advantage of his reprieve to record and analyze the feelings of an old man in order to throw further light on the image of himself that he intended to leave behind.

Soon after Gide's death, V. S. Pritchett wrote of him in *The New Statesman and Nation:* "One went to him as one goes to an interpreter who is familiar with several spiritual tongues; for the spell of a clear beguiling voice speaking the truth about himself. He was a natural traveller; but his best journeys were through his own life, which he displayed like some candid and figured landscape." Just because *So Be It* constitutes one more journey through his own life, it belongs, whatever the author himself thought, together with his monumental *Journals,* which Mr. Pritchett found "likely to rank as one of the great autobiographies of the West."

So Be It or *The Chips Are Down*—the alternate, rather flippant title reflects Gide's lack of solemnity about himself and his fate—represents the author's first truly posthumous work. For, if *Et nunc manet in te* (known in America as *Madeleine*) reached the world only after André Gide's death, he had nevertheless caused it to be issued as early as 1947 in a private edition. Yet it is significant that both these messages from beyond the grave, as Chateaubriand would have called them, are closely related to the *Journals*, which they prolong. It is fitting, therefore, that the present translation of *Ainsi soit-il* should be annotated as were the American and English editions of the *Journals* and of *Et nunc manet in te*. At least until such time as his many creative and critical works are universally accorded their due, Gide survives through his personal confessions—as he does also in the already numerous memoirs, eyewitness accounts, confessions, and indiscretions written by his close friends and bitter enemies who suffered the contagion of those *Journals*.

SO BE IT

OR

THE CHIPS ARE DOWN

I DON'T know what the result will be, but I have made up my mind to write at random. Difficult undertaking, for the pen (it's a fountain pen) falls behind thought. And it is essential not to foresee what one is going to say. But there is always an element of artifice in it. No matter how consciously one tries not to use the headlights, a sort of inner radar nonetheless sends out warnings. . . .

I have just crossed out four words; that's cheating. I'll try not to do so again. . . . Let me warn you at the outset: be careful not to give too much importance to what I am setting down now; that would simply play into Benda's hands.[1] If I feel like contradicting myself, I shall contradict myself without hesitation; I shall not strive for "coher-

---

[1] Julien Benda (1867–1955) was known for the uncompromising rationalism of his early attacks on Bergsonism and his condemnation of all modern literature for deviating from the Greco-Roman-Christian tradition of the dedicated intellectual. In his *Belphégor* (1919) and *La France byzantine* (1945) he aimed to prove that the aesthetics of French society in the first half of the twentieth century produced a literature of primarily emotional and sensational content signed by such as Proust, Gide, Valéry, Giraudoux, and the Surrealists.

ence." But shall not affect incoherence either. Beyond logic there is a sort of hidden psychology that is more important to me here. I take care to say "here," for I can endure illogicality only momentarily and for fun. To be sure, nothing is less laughable than an illogicality and I am aiming to amuse myself here. However, I recognize that without Descartes's rigorous reasoning nothing solid or lasting could have been established. But that cautious game is played on quite another level; for the moment it's not my concern. And perhaps at my age it is permissible to be a little free-and-easy. *Amen.* (Which means, I believe, so be it!)

I must have been about fourteen when I had my first taste of *horror*. It was in the Place Saint-Sulpice, which at that time was paved with stone blocks. A few yards from me a van passes. A boy, about twelve years old, has managed to get a free ride by perching on the rear of the vehicle where the driver can't see him. He has his fill of the ride, wants to get off, jumps, but catches his smock on something. So that, pulled backward in mid-jump, he falls and strikes his head on the pavement. Passers-by, having seen the accident, shout, wave, try to stop the driver, who has not seen anything

4

and whips his horse to a trot. The poor child's head bounces from paving-stone to paving-stone. Vainly he tries to protect it with his arms. But he must have lost consciousness almost at once. When the van comes to a stop thirty yards farther on (for someone has finally thrown himself at the horse's head), the child's face has become a sort of bloody pulp. . . .

(At that age, I think such an experience of horror made me greatly doubt the existence of God. Subsequently considerable effort was devoted to patching up in me the conception of divine providence. And on my own I had more or less succeeded in restoring it. Besides, this is not the plane on which it is—or that I feel it to be—most suspect.)

Since that time we have been so steeped in horror that a trivial incident like this may make people merely shrug their shoulders. "Not worth mentioning" [2] in the same breath with the atrocities of war, with that vast upsetting of all the values that constituted our reasons for living. . . .

I have made the acquaintance of a word that describes a condition from which I have been suffer-

---

[2] This expression occurs in English in the text.

ing for months—a very beautiful word: anorexia. From *an*, privative, and *orexis*, appetite. It means a lack of appetite ("which must not be confused with loathing," says Littré). This term is hardly used by any but doctors, but that doesn't matter; I need it. To say that I am suffering from anorexia is going too far; the worst of it is that I scarcely suffer from it at all. But my physical and intellectual want of appetite has become such that at times I don't really know what keeps me alive except the habit of living. It seems to me that to cease being I should merely have to let myself go. In what I am writing here, don't see despair, but rather *satisfaction*.

I am weighing each word I am writing, and should be vexed with myself for exaggerating my thought. After all, as for the game I was playing, I have won it. But I have ceased being really interested in it since Em. left me.[3] Since then it often seems to me that I have merely pretended to live; she was my reality. It doesn't matter if I fail to make myself understood. I don't altogether under-

---

[3] The abbreviation "Em." stands for Emmanuèle, the name Gide consistently used in his writings for his wife, Madeleine, who died on 17 April 1938. It is significant that the name Emmanuel is interpreted in the Bible as "God with us" and that "Em." is simply the pronunciation of "M." for Madeleine.

stand, myself. For instance, I don't really know what I mean by *reality*. For her, reality was a God in whom I could not believe. . . . I have ceased trying to understand anything whatever.

If what I have just written were to cause any young man who might read me to stumble or to lose any of his ardour, I should tear out these pages immediately. But I beg him to consider my age and to make an effort to realize that the age of eighty is not the time to try leaping forward—unless out of oneself. Let that young man look elsewhere, in my youthful writings, for invitations to joy, to that natural exaltation in which I lived so long; they are frequent. But at present I could not reassume them without affectation. It is affectation that makes so many of today's writings, often even the best among them, unbearable to me. The author takes on a tone that is not natural to him. That is what I should like to avoid. Sincerity must precede the choice of words and the rhythm of the sentence; it has nothing to do with the cynicism of confessions. It has no worse or more perfidious enemy than self-satisfaction, which comes along and distorts everything. One cannot be too severe toward oneself; but this requires long and patient practice.

I should not like to rejoice either in that anorexia I have just spoken about. Yesterday, in Cabris, where I had gone from Nice to see the Herbarts, I suddenly felt that, after all, I could still feel happy to be alive and declared this at once to Pierre and Elisabeth and to Mme Théo, who is three or four years older than I.[4] The four of us were sitting under an arbour, not so thick but what we could see recurrent touches of deep-blue sky between the broad vine leaves. The bunches of grapes hanging here and there were swelling for the approaching vintage. The air was both warm and soft. I had come bringing good news—in particular the news of the reprinting of my *Faux-Monnayeurs*.[5] The book has been chosen among the twelve best novels selected for a new collection that sounds as if it will be rather important. Pierre and Elisabeth told

---

[4] Pierre Herbart (1903–   ), the novelist and journalist, accompanied André Gide to Russia in 1936. His wife, Elisabeth, is the daughter of the Belgian painter Théo Van Rysselberghe (1862–1926). Mme Van Rysselberghe (1865–   ), whom Gide most often called simply "Mme Théo" or *"la petite dame,"* has outlived Gide.

[5] In 1950 a jury composed of Gérard Bauër, Roland Dorgelès, Emile Henriot, and André Maurois chose *The Counterfeiters* (*The Coiners* in England), originally published in 1926, as one of the twelve best novels of the first half of the twentieth century to be reprinted in a special collection by Editions Le Prat.

8

me how pleased they were to see its rightful place granted at last to a work which all (or almost all) agreed to consider abortive at the moment of its publication. Simply it didn't correspond to what the critics had decreed the rules of the genre to be. But here, as on so many other occasions, I won on appeal the action that was brought against me then. It will be the same for *Corydon* and for *Saül*.[6] As for *Les Caves du Vatican*, I am awaiting with joyful impatience the test of its presentation at the Comédie-Française this autumn.[7] Indeed, it is one of the few causes for curiosity that still bind me to life. . . .

From beginning to end, the whole affair was unexpected. I had let Heyd reprint in Volume VII (I believe) of my *Théâtre complet* (quite surprised to see him find enough to fill so many volumes) an adaptation of the "*sotie*" that I had made at the re-

[6] When it appeared in 1924, *Corydon* shocked because of its plea for an understanding of homosexuality; but as time went on Gide came to think of it as "the most important" of his books. The play *Saul* suffered from its insistence on the same theme. Written before 1900 and published in 1903, it was not produced until 1922. Yet the author frequently spoke of it as one of the best of his works.

[7] Classified by the author as a *sotie* or moral farce, *Les Caves du Vatican* (1914) is really a novel. It is known in English as *Lafcadio's Adventures* and *The Vatican Swindle*, but *The Roman Underground* might be more appropriate.

9

quest of the "Bellettriens" of Lausanne;[8] then I had not thought of it again . . . until the day (it was last summer) when a cordial letter from Touchard, the very likable present Administrator of the Comédie-Française, sought me out at Juan-les-Pins, where I was languishing at the moment. (And, truly, I was in the doldrums.) Jean Meyer, he informed me, had just discovered the play, had immediately read it aloud to the "Sociétaires" of the theater, who had unanimously accepted it with the intention of staging that farce as soon as possible—that is, by the following autumn.[9] I accepted joyfully. However, certain passages had to be gone

---

[8] André Gide made his stage adaptation of *Les Caves du Vatican* in 1933 for a series of productions given in December of that year in Montreux, Lausanne, and Geneva by the "Belles Lettres" Society of young actors. He called it a three-act farce. It was published in 1948 by Ides et Calendes of Neuchâtel in Volume V of *Le Théâtre complet d'André Gide* with a dedication to Richard Heyd, the editor and publisher of the plays.

[9] All French writers are susceptible to the honor of being played by the national Comédie-Française (founded by Louis XIV and subsidized by the state), which frequently adds new plays to its vast repertory of classical and modern drama. Its principal actors (officially elected by their peers to the temporary status of "Pensionnaires" and later to the permanent one of "Sociétaires") choose their productions through a reading-committee of their own presided over by the Administrator. A Sociétaire since 1942, Jean Meyer often directs new productions besides acting in them. Pierre-Aimé Touchard was Administrator from 1947 to 1953.

over. I promised to get to it at once. And a few months later Jean Meyer (who planned to play the role of Protos) came to Taormina, where together we finished polishing the whole thing. He was satisfied with the few scenes I had composed in the meantime, which were to give greater importance to the heroine's role.

For, even though I already suffered from that anorexia (on which I haven't said all I wish to say), although I feel old and already as if *obsolete*, I do not think my intellectual faculties have diminished much; so that that occasion was enough to start them off again. And now I am waiting in Nice for Touchard's call, very eager to be present at the first tryouts, when each actor makes his first contact with his role—knowing that it is too late to intervene when habits have already been formed.

I told Jean Meyer what had taken place for *Perséphone* when, invited by Ida Rubinstein to her charming private house in the Place des Etats-Unis, I came up against the perfect agreement among Ida, Stravinsky, and Copeau, all neophytes, and Barsacq, the producer, who naturally fell into step.[1]

---

[1] An "opera" in three tableaux (really a sort of ballet-cantata), Gide's *Perséphone* was written for Ida Rubinstein, with

"You see," my friend Copeau said, "there is no question of presenting the action itself to the public. We must proceed through allusions."

"Yes," Stravinsky exclaimed, "it's like the Mass. And that's what I like about your play. The action itself must be implied. . . ."

"So I got the idea," Copeau continued, "that everything could take place in a single place, thanks to a narrator who would just give a recital, a reflection, of the facts themselves. Everything in a single place: a temple or, even better, a cathedral. . . ."

I felt lost, for Ida and Stravinsky tried to outdo each other in their approval.

"But, Jacques," I still tried to object, "don't forget that I clearly indicated for the first act: a seashore . . ."

"Yes, the narrator will make that clear."

"It's wonderful," Ida said.

"And the second act, which is to take place in Hades. How in your cathedral . . ."

"But *we have the crypt,*" Copeau continued with

---

whom Jacques Copeau collaborated on the staging; Igor Stravinsky composed the music and Kurt Joos arranged the choreography. André Barsacq was the producer when Ida Rubinstein declaimed and mimed the title role for the first time at the Théâtre de l'Opéra on 30 April 1934.

12

such assurance that, that very evening, giving up the game, I set out for Syracuse to see again the ancient setting that I just happened to want.

I believe that Stravinsky found it very hard to forgive me for not being present at the first playing of his very beautiful score, but that was beyond my strength. The music was appreciated, I think. As for the very subject of the drama, the public understood nothing, of course. If ever anyone takes it into his head to revive that "ballet" (and Stravinsky's score deserves such interest), I beg the producer to follow closely the indications I gave. If the actress's voice carries a little more than Rubinstein's did (which, I am told, did not reach beyond the seventh row), I feel sure of its success.[2]

People were very unjust toward Ida Rubinstein.[3] The ballerina in her harmed the tragic actress, as did that vast fortune she often displayed stupidly.

~~~~~~~~

[2] André Gide was right, for *Perséphone* has come to be considered among Stravinsky's greatest works. In 1957 two recordings of this work appeared simultaneously, one conducted by Stravinsky with Vera Zorina in the title role and the other conducted by André Cluytens with Claude Nollier as Perséphone.

[3] Russian-born Ida Rubinstein danced with the Ballets Russes of Diaghilev and staged performances of her own in works by D'Annunzio, Valéry, Gide, etc. It was she who commissioned Gide to adapt *Antony and Cleopatra*, which she staged at the Paris Opera in 1920.

13

Those who, like me, were fortunate enough to hear her in the fourth act of *Phèdre* (on the occasion of a single "charity" performance at the Sarah Bernhardt Theatre) can testify that she was incomparable. I don't think I ever heard the alexandrines recited so well as by her. Never had Racine's lines seemed to me more beautiful, more panting, richer in hidden potentiality. And nothing, either in her costume or in her attitudes, ran counter to that extraordinary and almost superhuman harmony. . . . All that sinks into the past. Decidedly, I do not like the theater; it involves too many concessions to the public, and the factitious always wins out over the authentic, adulation over sincere praise. The actor inclines too readily to prefer Sardou to Racine, and the applause of the mass of uncultivated to that of the small number of experts. But let us call a halt; I should have too much to say on this subject.[4] I come back to anorexia.

I am not much interested in the joys of eating;

----

[4] On various occasions Gide had already expressed himself in this regard. Even before his brilliant lecture of 1904, "The Evolution of the Theater," he had noted in his *Journals* for 1902: "The habit of playing mediocre dramatists makes the actor see his contribution as too important. He therefore uses the same artifice in presenting Racine's pure gold as in foisting upon us Sardou's tin-plate."

less and less; satisfied after a dozen mouthfuls; probably somewhat hard to please as to the quality of butter and of bread; as for the meat, if it is stringy or badly cooked, I prefer going without dinner. Even the best wine I like just as well when cut with water; even better; *à la française,* as Montaigne says, though it scandalize my friends. When I am alone at least, I flee famous restaurants.

I have had to accept the facts: I am miserly by nature (I must get that from my Norman ancestors), but despite that, I see generosity in me. Understand if you can. . . . And yet, I think the explanation is rather simple: for myself, for my own comfort, I shrink from expenditure. Moreover, with age I have changed somewhat; at the invitation of physical weakness, I am treating myself with greater regard. Besides, I am so deficient in the sense of the value of money that I often lay out thousand-franc notes when hundred-franc notes would do. But I planned to talk of anorexia.

That lack of appetite is as much intellectual as physical. I have great trouble in getting interested in what I am reading. After twenty pages the new book falls from my hands, and I go back to Vergil, who no longer provides me any surprise exactly, but at least a constant delight.

This condition is very recent, and I can hardly recognize myself in it. Yes, until close to my eightieth year I had managed to maintain in me (and quite naturally; I mean without any artifice) a sort of curiosity, of almost frisky cheerfulness, which I portrayed as best I could in my books, which made me spring forward toward everything that seemed to me worthy of love and admiration, despite the mortifications. The inhibition I feel today comes neither from the outer world nor from others, but from myself. Through sympathy I long kept myself in a state of fervour. When I travel, I do so with a young companion and live by proxy. I adopt his wonders and joys. . . . I think I should still be capable of some of them. But it is myself that I am becoming progressively less interested in and breaking away from. Yet I still remain very sensitive to the sight of adolescence. Moreover, I have taken care not to let my desires slumber, listening to the advice of Montaigne, who is particularly wise on this score. He knew, and I know too, that wisdom does not lie in renunciation, in abstinence, and took care not to let that secret spring dry up too soon, even going so far as to encourage himself toward physical pleasure, if I grasp his meaning.

. . . Nonetheless, my anorexia comes partly, comes especially, from a withdrawal of the sap, I am forced to admit. Even at the age of eighty one is not inclined to admit such things. King David was probably about my age when he invited the very young Abishag to come and warm his couch. That passage, like many another in the Bible, would seriously embarrass commentators if they were not able to look for, and find, a mystical interpretation in it—which is not obvious to me.

Anorexia. To overcome it, at least momentarily, I needed only these few pages I have just written as fast as I could. To me idleness is unendurable. Translating *Arden of Feversham* with Elisabeth H. for Jean-Louis Barrault, I was happy.[5] Even happier when composing for Jean Meyer the few supplementary scenes of *Les Caves du Vatican;* more fit than ever. And now that I have resolved to let my pen follow its fancy (though I do weigh the words I am writing), I again enjoy moments of utter felicity. I am not rereading myself, and shall wait until later to find out the worth of what I have

---

[5] Gide's adaptation of the Elizabethan play once attributed to Shakespeare, *Arden of Feversham,* has never been published or produced.

just written. This is an experiment I have never before tried, for ordinarily I carry the least project in my head for months and years. If I had my life to begin over again, I should grant myself greater license. But had I slackened the reins, I might perhaps have done nothing worth while. It took me a very long time to realize to what an extent my heredity tied me down. In other and simpler words: I was much less free than I thought I was, extraordinarily held down, held in check, held back by the feeling of *duty*. To how many invitations I now regret not having yielded! For my greater enrichment, doubtless; but perhaps also for the dissolution of my character. . . . But it is futile to try to reckon this.

Many novelists or dramatists never succeed in giving their characters' remarks an authentic ring. Corneille's feat consists in getting his listener to the point of forgoing such a thing. I reread *Horace* last night, and was almost dumbfounded. The great mistake for the tragic writer would be trying to make his declamation sound natural. He gets away with it only through style: everything must be transposed onto the superhuman plane. But the

proportions must be maintained, so that everything becomes art and nothing seems artificial.

Corneille's language is so beautiful that I don't
really have to force my admiration, but I find it
hard to convince myself of the benefit that such a
plunge into the artificial can bring to a young
mind. Furthermore, it is not just the same, by exception, with the *Cid*, where the adolescent's enthusiasm may be sincere. But with Corneille he is
often urged to a conventional admiration that the
teacher must explain and motivate; there is nothing
spontaneous left in it. It is an initiation to the artificial, and I am not sure that the child's mind has
much to gain from this. And after that the child
runs the risk of equating *artificial* with *literature*.
All this to say that I do not consider Corneille, always and everywhere, to be a very good teacher.

How I like the disposition of the modest country
priest who, during a procession organized in the
hope that a disastrous drought would end (I think
it is what is known as a "rogation"), holds out his
hand and, feeling a few drops of water, exclaims:
"Why . . . it's raining! What a happy coincidence!" A candid soul like that of the Anglican

minister made famous, as Dorothy Bussy told me,[6] by an apostrophe to his flock: "Yes, brethren," he exclaimed, "there is but one God," then added as he was carried away by his enthusiasm: "But one God, as there is but one sun, but one moon, and a multitude of stars." This has even more flavor in English.

I am still very fond of witty remarks and anecdotes, despite those who see in such an admission a sign of my mind's incurable frivolity. But how rare are those who can repeat such witticisms without deforming them! I was planning to make a collection of them, but I should have excluded from it many of those famous remarks, of those quasi-historic apothegms, obviously made up later on, that I cannot really believe wholly.

But some of those remarks are strangely revealing, and I should not forgive myself if I failed to preserve them. This by Péguy, for instance:

Eve, that "calm lump," has just appeared, to the utter consternation of the subscribers to the *Cahiers*.[7] Cancellations pour in. It's a calamity. Péguy

---

[6] The sister of Lytton Strachey and wife of the painter Simon Bussy, Dorothy Bussy translated into English most of André Gide's novels.

[7] This incident occurred in 1913. Charles Péguy (1873–1914), essayist and poet, exerted a great influence through his

strides up and down the studio of our common friend Paul-Albert Laurens, who is pretending to paint. Péguy is silent. Some claimed that Péguy had been writing *Eve* for some time. . . . But I can assert that that gigantic and monotonous poem was written (I dare not say *improvised*) to thwart a volume of verse by Lucas de Pesloüan. I know this, for the volume of verse was given me by Péguy himself for my judgment. Lucas de Pesloüan was one of the chief financial backers of the *Cahiers* and a most faithful friend, but his poetry was appallingly bad—in my categorical opinion, unpublishable. In vain Péguy was looking for a proper reason to reject it. He thought he had found a valid objection by setting up against it a volume of verse of his own, to which it was natural that he should grant preference, and which was to surfeit the subscribers to the *Cahiers* with poetry for a long time to come. But of that book nothing was yet written. It was essential to get down to it at once. And when Péguy got down to it . . . the result was *Eve*.

fortnightly periodical, *Les Cahiers de la Quinzaine,* published from 1900 to 1914 from his own bookshop across from the Sorbonne. The painter Paul-Albert Laurens, one of Gide's closest friends, had traveled with Gide in Tunisia and Algeria on the first memorable trip of 1893.

Nonetheless, Péguy was worried—somewhat as Mallarmé was, after *Un Coup de dès,* when he asked Valéry: "Tell me, I beg you, as a friend. . . . In your opinion, is it the work of a madman?" Most likely, Péguy had no doubts about himself, about his genius . . . but still, that poem that kept on marking time? "In it I portrayed the Good Lord. . . ." Yes, to be sure; it's a stagnant subject. Hence, nothing annoyed Péguy so much as certain articles in which critics dared to mention a parallel between *Eve* and the *Divine Comedy.* As if between this and that the least connection could be established! He went about muttering between his teeth: "Dante! . . . Dante! . . ." And suddenly he stops and strikes the table with his fist; he has discovered what he wanted to say: "Dante! . . . Their Dante is a mere tourist!" Dare I add that I consider this remark wonderful? To be sure, in Péguy's eyes, Dante, in his excursion through hell, must have looked like a "globe-trotter." [8]

Equally authentic was Péguy's outburst when he was blamed for being unjust to Laudet in *Un Nouveau Théologien* (one of his best pamphlets).[9]

---

[8] In English in the text.

[9] Almost all of Péguy's prose writings, which he published himself in his *Cahiers,* were pamphlet-like. *A New Theologian*

"Remember the recommendation of Christ himself: Judge not," he was told. Whereupon Péguy protested: "But I am not judging; I am condemning." Romain Rolland has spoken excellently of Péguy. André Rousseaux, on the other hand, speaks as a Catholic and addresses himself to Catholics; nothing is more likely to distort judgment.[1]

I feel—or rather, I know—that I have not much longer to live. I remind myself of this at every minute in the day. Pains and pangs may come, but they have been spared me up to now. Yet my heart is weak . . . (I smoke too much). After twenty paces, I am out of breath. I hope to die without ado, as simply as if going to sleep. Is it possible? Above all, without anything theatrical about it. Without forewarning. Without preparations.

There was a time, a very long time, when treasures would not have counterbalanced a beautiful sentence in my esteem. Now I write any old way and aim only to be natural. This is not, properly

of 1911 treats many of his favorite themes: Christianity and atheism, the place of the humanities in the modern world, war and peace, Joan of Arc.

[1] Romain Rolland's *Péguy* in two volumes came out in 1945, André Rousseaux's *Le Prophète Péguy*, likewise in two volumes, in 1942–4.

speaking, a book that I am writing here. Without
any definite plan or outline, I am progressing aim-
lessly, ready to tear up whatever strikes me as too
amorphous or too preposterous. I shall see later on.
Meanwhile, I take care not to reread what I have
written. Besides, I do not always dislike the preposterous; I consider it often revealing of various
impulses that we generally take care to force into a
pattern. But that kind of preposterous must be almost unconscious; it must escape one. In this way I
wrote, the year before last, a few pages with which
I confess to having been particularly pleased. I
had called it *L'Arbitraire*.[2] Yes, indeed, I had let
my pen follow its whim. My traveling-companions
(Richard Heyd, my son-in-law, and my daughter)
had set out from the Swiss-Italian border for a
short trip to Venice.[3] They had left me alone at
Ponte-Tresa. They were to be gone three days. Not
the least distraction. It was raining. So, I had sat

[2] The ten-page beginning of a preposterous unfinished story
that Gide entitled "The Arbitrary One" or "The Bitrary. Art"
(if it was he who spelled the title as *L'Art bitraire*) is appropriately dated at the end: "April first 1947."

[3] Catherine Gide was married in August 1946 to the writer
Jean Lambert (1914–   ). Richard Heyd founded the publishing-house Ides et Calendes at Neuchâtel, which brought
out many of Gide's late works. Ponte-Tresa, a few miles from
Lugano, stands on the Swiss-Italian border.

down at the table in an ordinary hotel parlour, in front of a blank sheet of paper, with my mind made up to write anything whatever so long as it made no sense. The result seems to me rather good.

How often I have longed to write a book that would completely disregard my past, that people would try in vain to link up with what is pompously called *my work*. It's no good; I fall back into the themes already gone over, which I don't think I can still turn to account. I feel much more disposed to laughter than I was in my youth. I then took seriously many a "problem" that makes me smile or laugh today. I make an exception for the political, social, or economic problems that concern others in an often tragic way, but I think of those I used to imagine, often quite gratuitously, between man and the divinity. It seems to me now that most often it is all pure invention, and that the best is to carry on without paying too much attention to it. Whence the serious accusation of "despiritualizing" myself that has been made against me. Some, who wished me well, have claimed that as a result of my former concerns some secret unrest was still tormenting me, that my serenity was but pretense, that neither the Devil nor God was the loser; that, moreover, relieved of my unrest, I thereby relinquished all justification and all value. "Henceforth, how can this corpse mean much to us?" Mauriac exclaimed.[4] He was kind enough to add that, if I were utterly sincere, I should admit that . . . This is wallowing in the imaginary. I think I have explained myself fully on that score.

All the same, there would be pretense in depicting myself as more frivolous than I am. I have trouble taking *myself* seriously, rather than others. Give one's life for others? . . . Yes, perhaps. For a cause? . . . We have too often been fooled.

I have a great regard for integrity. The moment fiction is not involved, I cling to the truth. Thus, in reporting on French Equatorial Africa, I related nothing that was not scrupulously exact.[5] And likewise in the account of my relations with Wilde.[6] The latter embarrassed some, who felt offended by my assertions. A pamphlet appeared in England

---

[4] The novelist François Mauriac (1885–   ) probably wrote this in one of his articles for *Le Figaro*.

[5] Various polemics resulted from Gide's exposing the abuses of the big concessionary companies in his *Voyage au Congo* (1927), translated as *Travels in the Congo*.

[6] Gide speaks frequently of Wilde in his writings, but his first major study was the memorial essay of 1901, written a year after Oscar Wilde's death, and his most disturbing revelations appeared in his memoirs, *Si le grain ne meurt . . .* of 1926 (translated as *If It Die*).

26

entitled *The Abominable Lies of André Gide*,
which claimed to demolish my accounts.[7] Subsequently this allowed certain biographers to pay no
attention to my testimony. I protest that I invented
nothing, absolutely nothing, and that everything I
tell in this connection is altogether and utterly
exact. But how can one fail to admit in advance
that Wilde confided intimately only in those who
shared his tastes? With all others, he had to pretend and resort to deceit. With many of his biographers a portion of his life is left out—perhaps the
most important part. Believing him is almost tantamount to a personal confession. No matter how
devoted some of his friends may have been, it was
only after they turned their backs that Wilde began to live.

Time often helped me out, and in many disputes
my opponent withdrew without my needing to record his collapse. This is what took place for
Maurras, for Massis, for Béraud, and for Montfort.[8] The same will probably be true for Charles

---

[7] This anonymous pamphlet seems to have left no trace in
bibliographies.

[8] Before becoming famous as the founder of the nationalist
movement known as *Action française,* Charles Maurras (1868–
1952) defended his friend Maurice Barrès (1862–1923),
whose doctrine of the necessity of rooting oneself in one's na-

Du Bos, who would be considerably embarrassed today, I am convinced, by many of his statements.[9] He was too basically fair not to realize that he had gone astray; and even in certain conversations after the publication of his book, he didn't hide his regrets from me. One day before finishing the writing of that book he asked me to come to his house on the Ile Saint-Louis. He had no very definite idea about pederasty and needed explanations. The conversation was frightfully painful. Uranism was not the only thing that Charlie did not understand; the same could be said of life in general. For him everything was or became abstract, intellectual. It is impossible to imagine such an absence of contact

tive soil had been attacked by Gide. Gide debated with Maurras at length about the strengthening of plants through uprooting and transplantation, for Maurras had ventured to speak of poplars without foreseeing that Gide the gentleman farmer would worst him in a most amusing argument. The real offensive against Gide's "satanic" influence did not begin until after the First World War, with the articles of Henri Massis. (1886–), a Catholic critic identified with the nationalism of Maurras; Henri Béraud (1885–1958), who directed his attacks against Gide and the Gide-inspired periodical, *La Nouvelle Revue Française;* and Eugène Montfort (1877–1936), who specialized in scathing criticism and spurious anecdotes.

[9] Long an intimate friend of Gide, the critic Charles Du Bos (1882–1939) turned against his friend in his *Dialogue avec André Gide* of 1929, written just after his reconversion to Catholicism.

with phenomena, with the outer world, with reality. I recognized the man who, unable to fill his fountain pens himself, used to carry a week's supply that he would go and have refilled at Smith's once a week; [1] the man who used to call a secretary to open or close a window; who at La Bastide, where he was working with Elisabeth Van Rysselberghe on the translation of Keats's letters, was worried as to how to put out an oil lamp. "I don't think I can do it. Give me a candle instead." The same man who asked her with an absolutely straight face where snails had their horns (because this came up in the English text)—"I must know: is it on the rear or on the front?" "What, Charlie, have you never seen snails?" "Perhaps, but I have never looked at them." [2] Yes, that was it. Charlie didn't look at anything, didn't inquire into anything except with an intellectual scrutiny. Consequently he had incomprehensible gaps. But inasmuch as he was then in a charming, playful mood, he used to laugh with us, and even more than we did, at his blunder. It seemed to me then that our

[1] Smith's is an English bookshop under the arcades of the rue de Rivoli.

[2] The same incident is recorded in *The Journals of André Gide*, III, 164, under date of 4 June 1931.

understanding was complete. Religious conversion came along and spoiled everything.

I read yesterday, in Renan's very discerning study of Lamennais (1857): "Nothing is so tiresome as Catholic polemics, for the apologist grants himself many advantages that the disinterested critic must refuse himself." Hence it is better to elude discussion. Many of my friends, and often the best of them, became converted.[3] I kept my affection for them, and it was often very keen, but I ceased talking with them. Why in the dickens did Charlie call his book *Dialogue avec André Gide*? When he crushes me with arguments, he does so in the name of a transcendent Truth that demolishes me in advance. Why, despite that indictment, does he continue to protest that he loves me dearly? A touch of lay equity would be more appropriate than that gush of affection in his conversation and his letters. The surprising thing is that during the

---

[3] Indeed, the number of Gide's friends who became converts to Roman Catholicism cannot fail to impress one. The poets Paul Claudel and Francis Jammes, the critics Henri Ghéon and Charles Du Bos, the close associates Jacques Copeau and Jacques Rivière are only the most striking cases. Gide's own spirituality and his extraordinary susceptibility to spiritual qualities in others partly explain the number of converts in his circle.

years of our frequentation he never showed me anything but that affection. Reservations and protests were revealed to me, all of a sudden, by his book. Henceforth I shall never again be astonished by anything from a devout person.

Man's relations to God always seemed to me much more important and interesting than the relations of men among themselves. Moreover, it was natural enough that, born into easy circumstances, I never had to be much concerned with the latter. If my parents had had to earn their living with difficulty, this would probably not have been true. My heredity and then my Protestant upbringing turned my mind almost exclusively toward moral problems. In those early years I had not yet grasped the fact that duties toward God and duties toward the self could be the same. At present I have a great tendency to confuse them, perhaps too completely. I am still exigent: much more toward myself than toward others, but have ceased to believe that there is anyone outside myself, any power superior to and independent of me, that does the exacting. To tell the truth, I no longer keep records, as I once did. I have ceased indulging, at night before trying to go to sleep, in what the Protestant calls *self-examination;* I act as if I

31

had passed the examination. And don't jump to the conclusion that this is a matter of pride. It sometimes, indeed often, happens that I am very little satisfied with myself: this is when I have let some mean impulse dictate my conduct. People have criticized my coquetry; the word is excessively degrading, but I don't know how else to refer to a certain concern not to tolerate disfiguring impulses in me for more than a very fleeting moment. I most certainly do not count among them the impulses of indignation, of revolt, even of hatred. Even further, I do not at all try to turn away from whatever may provoke them. On the contrary, I consider that it is good never to lose sight of the many reasons, alas, that the present world provides for urgent dissatisfaction. I merely mean that I will not tolerate that such dissatisfaction should alter a certain secret, deep serenity.

But as for declaring myself satisfied with the present state of affairs . . . no! that's asking too much of me. Everywhere I look, I see nothing but illegitimate favours and injustices, or that sort of complacent acceptance of the iniquity by those who don't have to suffer from it personally. . . . I hope I never write on this subject any of those

high-sounding phrases which would make me smile
or blush a few months later. With what enthusiasm
I read Lamennais's *Paroles d'un croyant* at the age
of eighteen! [4] The very same enthusiasm with
which Lamennais had written the book, and with
what an authentic conviction! I recently opened
the book again—complete collapse. . . . In the
notebook in which I had begun writing again, at
random rather as I am doing here, and which I
lost at Rapallo, I had related the lynching of a very
young German parachutist at the beginning of the
war. It took place in a village through which we
happened to pass the next day. The furious peas-
ants had thrashed him, beaten him black and blue
with shovels and rakes until he died, without being
able to get anything from that obstinate youth but
a stubborn *"Heil Hitler!"* Such nonetheless authentic martyrs, such zealots of divergent doctrines, are
most embarrasing, to be sure. One wonders at the
gate of what other paradise what other Saint Peter
will meet them . . . And what other Pascal will

----

[4] *The Words of a Believer* (1833) by Félicité-Robert de
Lamennais (1782–1854) is a collection of Biblical-seeming
verses expressing love of the oppressed and hatred of social
injustice on the part of a priest in revolt against Rome.

dare to write: "I am inclined to believe those who get killed for . . ." (or something similar).[5]

I caught myself yesterday wondering with the greatest possible seriousness whether I was still really alive. The outer world was there, and I perceived it clearly; but was it really I perceiving it? At the time of my initiation to German metaphysics, I remained for some time dazzled by Schopenhauer's remark: "Hence I am the support of the whole world. . . ." I recall it very well, after more than a half-century; [6] nothing existed except in relation to me. It was intoxicating. Now the question was turned about: without my help everything existed and continued to be. The world had no need of me. And during a rather long time (it lasted about a quarter of an hour) *I absented myself;* it seemed to me that I had ceased to be here; and my disappearance went unnoticed. Then I realized that I was the one, nevertheless, who was aware

---

[5] In his *Pensées* (IX, 593 in the Brunschvicg edition), Pascal says: "I believe only those stories for the truth of which the witnesses would be willing to lay down their lives." His mention of China in the preceding lines indicates that he was thinking of the missionaries slaughtered by the Chinese.

[6] I was eighteen. [Note supplied by the author in the French edition. Such notes will hereafter be indicated by an A. in brackets.]

and who was telling myself: I am not here. I returned to fill my place, but as if dumfounded.

I no longer have any great curiosity as to what life may still bring me. I have said more or less well what I had to say, and fear repeating myself. But idleness is a burden to me. Yet the thing that would keep me from killing myself (although I do not at all consider suicide reprehensible) is that some would try to see in that deed a sort of confession of failure, the obligatory result of my error. Others would assume that I was giving Grace the slip. It would be hard to convince people that, simply, I am surfeited with living and don't know how to use the little time left me. Anorexia. The hideously inexpressive face of Boredom.

I am especially disheartened by the concentric character of anything I might still undertake. . . . Oh, how hard it is to age well! You would like to do a favour for others, and you feel yourself becoming a burden. I can no longer do without the assistance (I was about to say the "help") of others. Where can I take refuge this winter? Once the rehearsals and the showing of *Les Caves du Vatican* (from which it must be admitted that I am expecting the keenest pleasure) are over, I can see nothing beyond. Last year, that daily work with Elisabeth, that translation of *Arden of Feversham* which Jean-Louis Barrault had asked of me, was a wonderful resource. I do not yet feel any slackening of my intellectual faculties, but for what shall I use them? Examples of old age bringing disgrace are numerous. Heredia used to talk of some of them. I don't really know whether or not what he said of Musset should be believed. According to him (but I don't think he was inventing), every evening Musset sought in absinthe a sort of stupid forgetfulness. He would remain alone at his table on the terrace of the Café de la Régence (?) in the Place du Théâtre-Français until the closing hour. The waiters would take in the tables and chairs. To get him up from the table, his still half-full glass had to be carried out onto the sidewalk. He would follow.

Lamartine (according to Heredia) sank into gluttony. I can still hear the account he used to give of a certain delegation of girls from Saint-Point (?) come to pay their respects to Lamartine. It was a sort of embassy invented to distract and somewhat revive the old poet, like those artificial ceremonies in the last years of the reign of Louis XIV to amuse and flatter the old king's insatiable pride. So, a procession of damsels is announced one morning to Lamartine. He is not ready to re-

ceive them. In haste he is laced into his corset and
decked out. He descends the staircase and heads
toward the doorstep, where compliments and bou-
quets await him. But, by a stroke of ill-luck, the
dining-room door was open, and through it he
could see the luncheon preparations—in particular, a huge chocolate pudding in the centre of the
table. Unable to resist, Lamartine rushes toward it,
and, before anyone can stop him, he smears it all
over his shirt front, his necktie, his frock coat. . . .
The girls had to be told: "The Count is not quite
well. He deeply regrets it, but he cannot receive
you." Is there any truth in this? I don't know. In
any case, if this is fabricated, I am not responsible.

But I can guarantee the authenticity of this,
which I saw with my own eyes:

During our prolonged stay in Rome shortly after
our marriage, my wife and I generally took our
meals in the little Ranieri (?) restaurant near the
Piazza di Spagna, the very one, I think, that
Stendhal already spoke of. We had rented a very
ordinary three-room apartment in the Piazza Bar-
berini. One day we deserted the Ranieri for a very
good restaurant in the Corso, near the Piazza Co-
lonna. We were no sooner seated than we saw
enter a majestic old man whose wonderful face

was as if surrounded with a halo of white hair. A little short perhaps, but his whole person was instinct with nobility, intelligence, and serenity. He seemed not to see anyone; all the waiters bowed as he passed. The headwaiter zealously leaned over the table where the Olympian had taken his place and noted the order; but twice when called back he returned and listened respectfully to some recommendation or other. Obviously, the guest was someone famous. We scarcely took our eyes from him, and hence noticed, as soon as he had the menu in his hands, an extraordinary change in the features of his handsome face. To place his order he had become a mere mortal again. Then motionless and rigid, though without showing any impatience, his aspect totally expressionless. He came to life again only when the dish he had ordered had been set before him; he immediately cast off his nobility, his dignity, everything that signified his superiority over the rest of mankind. It seemed as if Circe had touched him with her magic wand. Far from being noble, he no longer suggested anything even merely human. He leaned over his plate and it could hardly be said that he began to eat; he guzzled like a glutton, like a swine. It was Carducci.

At that time I had the keenest admiration for his poetry and prose; it mattered little to me that D'Annunzio's fame was eclipsing his (as it was, even more, Pascoli's).[7] The sight of that moral decay was only the more painful to me. However great a man one may be to begin with, ah! it is a thousand times better to be dead than to tolerate such a surrender, such a self-repudiation, I thought. And you may well characterize as coquetry the anxiety not to leave behind too disagreeable an image of oneself. It is not a matter of hiding one's warts from the public, but rather of preventing, in so far as possible, a moral disfigurement; not of making up to look beautiful but of being so. . . . Even so, the body has to play its part. . . .

Old Papa Espinas was someone I loved dearly.[8]

---

[7] Giosuè Carducci (1835–1907) was the poet of history and nationalism, whereas Giovanni Pascoli (1855–1912), who succeeded him in the chair of Italian literature at Bologna, was a Wordsworthian, intimist poet. The flamboyant virtuosity of Gabriele d'Annunzio (1863–1938) was more accessible to foreigners.

[8] Alfred Espinas (1844–1922) wrote two doctoral theses published in 1877, one on *Animal Societies* and the other in Latin entitled *De civitate apud Platonem qua fiat una*. Later he wrote on Descartes's moral philosophy, on economic doctrines, and on social philosophy in the eighteenth century. His son Pierre, a mining-engineer, married Gide's cousin Jeanne Gide.

He had conceived a strange affection for me, I never knew just why. The author of a remarkable book (find the exact title) on the social feeling of certain insects, he had then turned his attention to Plato and Greek wisdom. He could listen as well as he could talk (an extremely rare thing), and I was often quite surprised to see his thought precede mine on certain points on which I am generally granted but little credit. An attack suddenly got the better of that keen intelligence. Overnight he became merely a wretched, crippled body suffering painfully which had to rely constantly on the care and attention that his very devoted wife showered upon him. It was expected that he would give in at any moment; it was even hoped for, since he had become but a rag, and hard to please at that, and Mme Espinas was at the end of her tether. It must be added that the old couple was in a most precarious financial situation; furthermore, neither of them would hear of a nurse, for Mme Espinas was to be equal to anything. Now, to the utter amazement and consternation of the children and friends, it was not he but she who died. Papa Espinas's faculties were so diminished that he was not aware of his loss. He merely realized that someone in their little apartment had just died, and thought vaguely that that person could only be he.

From my aunt Charles Gide I have the account of the funeral ceremony that brought together the intimate friends who intended to follow the procession to the cemetery. Old Espinas, quite incapable of taking part in anything, had been relegated to a small room under special supervision. And with a minimum of display the Protestant ritual was proceeding when suddenly, drowning out the discreet murmur of the prayers, could be heard from the next room the thundering voice of old Espinas furiously shouting: "Dead or alive, I still have to eat." Quickly something was brought to calm him, while everyone pretended not to have heard.

If I had my life to begin over again and it were possible for me to dispose of it at will, from the way I see things today I should probably give more time to work (I mean, to that of my education) but surely more time to adventure. I find it hard to console myself for not knowing Greek, for not speaking English and German fluently, and especially for having been so wary—a thing that doesn't jibe with my instinctive scorn of comfort. Dare I add in my own defense that my wife gave very little encouragement to my venturesome undertak-

ings, which immediately struck her as foolhardy?
She foresaw dangers everywhere. I don't yet understand, even today, how and where I often found
the strength to override her objections despite all
my love and my fear of hurting her. Listening too
much to that fear, I realized in time, would have
meant failure. Yet she took the greatest care not to
hinder my impulses and to show me constantly
that she wished not to influence my will or thought
in any way. But how could I have failed to feel,
through her very silences, her constant desire to
see me turn back? The sexual problem was eventually added to all that; but I think it was not an
essential part of the issue. Nevertheless, as it could
not be solved through mere submission, I believe it
pushed me along the path of revolt much more
rapidly and farther than I should have gone by
myself. Oh, let's not go back over that again.[9]

~~~~~~~~~~

[9] In the posthumously published account of his marital relations, Gide noted: "She was afraid of everything, even before
being afraid of me; and certainly that fear was increased by
the awareness of her fragility. I suggested to her as a motto:
leo est in via or *latet anguis in herba.*" And in his *Journals* for
9 September 1940 he wrote: "If I had listened to my own advice (I mean: the man I once was, listening to the one I am
today), I should have gone around the world four times . . .
and I should never have married. As I write these words, I
shudder as at an act of impiety. This is because I have re-

There is no use in recrimination and in dwelling on all one might have done. When I do occasionally get angry, I do so with myself, and this is what makes me advise the young over and over to tell themselves constantly and to convince themselves that most often it is up to them alone. It was up to me alone to travel in China, to me alone not to return constantly to the same places and wrap myself in landscapes and circumstances that had nothing further to teach me, simply through laziness, through inertia. . . . This is another piece of advice I give to the young, and the fact that I did not always follow it myself only adds to my assurance: know how to consider as preferable what costs you the most effort. . . . Yet I recognize that I demanded much of myself; and there are few things I resent so much, in old age, as having to relax on this score, having to pay attention to my powers and having constantly to note that they are deplorably limited; feeling, having to admit that I am no longer good for much.

. . .

mained nevertheless very much in love with what most held me in check and cannot affirm that that very check did not get the best out of me." These passages should be confronted with the most penetrating summary that Jean Schlumberger gives in his *Madeleine et André Gide* (1956), pp. 248–51.

I once wrote, I don't know now just where,[1] that I was certainly not indifferent to the fate of the world after I should cease to be here to suffer from or to enjoy it. This is true, and I have often shown myself (or more precisely pretended) to be more optimistic than I was in reality. Some days, if I let myself go, I should scream with despair. But a few glimmers of true virtue, self-sacrifice, nobility, and dignity are enough to obliterate the discouraging accumulation of stupidity, gluttony, and abjection. The sparks of virtue seem to me more dazzling by contrast. And I am willing to admit that, without them, our sorry world would be but an incoherent tissue of absurdities. But there they are, nevertheless, and I intend to count on them.

It is only too easy to indulge in oratory on this subject. And you have only to sprinkle it with mysticism to see gather around you an angelic choir, animated with excellent intentions and ready to quote edifying verses from the Gospels allowing no room for doubt as to the timeliness of your conversion. A certain number of my former friends, and among the best of them, became converted. Without having exactly broken off with

---

[1] Chiefly in *Les Nouvelles Nourritures* of 1935 (*New Fruits of the Earth*).

them, I was immediately convinced that conversation with them had become impossible. Any subject that was dear to me had to be cautiously avoided. It didn't seem to me that their conversion notably improved their characters; on the contrary, their worst shortcomings drew encouragement from being henceforth consecrated to God. Copeau, Jammes, Claudel, Ghéon [2] (I am citing only those who declared themselves openly) even buttressed their arrogance from that moment forth with a sort of conceit that quickly made them unbearable to me. Backed by the Church, they *couldn't* be wrong. *I* was the arrogant one for refusing to give in, to subordinate my own thought to what had been acknowledged as true, etc. . . . Subsequently I recognized the same collective conceit among the Communists, though on a quite different plane. Both groups taught me something, demonstrating the value of the individual by their irrational claims.

[2] Among his friends who became converts, Gide mentions particularly those he had known from rather early years. In his *Journals* for 5 March 1929 he had noted: "I would not swear that at a certain period of my life I was not very close to being converted. Thank God, a few converts among my friends took care of this, however. Jammes, or Claudel, or Ghéon, or Charlie Du Bos will never know how instructive their example was for me."

I am well aware that the problem barely begins at this point; for *Vae soli*. . . .[3] I was accused of trying to distinguish myself. My mind is as little inclined to controversy as a mind can be. Instead of standing up to my opponent, I wear myself out trying to understand him. It always seems to me that between men of good faith equally concerned with the public welfare there must eventually be agreement. But *they* are not of good faith, as I am reluctantly obliged to admit.—Are you now speaking of Communists or Catholics?—In the beginning I was thinking only of the latter, then let myself be carried away; because it is as true for the one group as it is for the other the moment they believe that *the end justifies the means*. From that specious doctrine have been born, and are born even today, the most abominable errors. Bad faith consists in pretending to lay one's cards on the table while keeping the winning trumps up one's sleeve. What is the use of discussing in such a case? You merely waste your ink, your time, and your patience. The only thing to do is to carry on and to act as if it were nothing. Yet I am confident that the publication of my correspondence with Jammes, with

---

[3] ". . . woe to him that is alone . . ." *Ecclesiastes*, iv, 10.

Claudel, with Charles Du Bos, and, even more, of Du Bos's *Journal*, will bear sufficient witness to . . . what each individual wants to see in those documents. In any event, I know what *I* see in those papers today when I happen to reread them.[4]

How much I liked Paul Laurens,[5] that brotherly friend, one of the most ardent of the converts, an associate of Péguy, but often shocked by the peremptory tone and stubborn excesses of certain attacks: "No, not at all!" he would say. "I know André Gide well; I assure you that it's not at all the same with him." He, at least, never made the least effort to "convert" me.

A noteworthy remark is attributed to Richepin:[6] "Each of us resembles his bust." How true that is!

[4] The correspondence between Francis Jammes and André Gide, extending from 1893 to 1938, was published in 1948; that between Paul Claudel and Gide, extending from 1899 to 1926, came out in 1949. On giving me these two volumes, a year apart, André Gide wrote in each one "for your edification"; this would seem to indicate his view of them. The correspondence with Charles Du Bos appeared in 1950 and the *Journal* of Du Bos, in which Gide's name appears on almost every page during certain years, began appearing in 1946.

[5] For the reasons given here, Gide never considered his old friend Paul-Albert Laurens in the same category with the other converts to Catholicism.

[6] Jean Richepin (1849–1926) was a facile poet and dramatist.

Rare indeed is the artist who shows no concern at all in life for the figure he cuts. However great a writer Suarès was,[7] he was petty enough to make a great point of never letting himself be seen except to his advantage. You had to give warning before ringing at his door, leaving him time to arrange the lightning and pull himself together. But what charm then, when he let himself go, when he deigned to forget himself! There was no more alert, vivacious, profound conversationalist than he. But so susceptible that the least remark (he saw everything in terms of himself) in which he could suspect some doubtful intention would make him retire within himself. He was always inclined to imagine a faction and plots against him. Despite all Rivière's efforts to reassure him, to convince him that the *N.R.F.*[8] was altogether favorable to him

---

[7] Poet, essayist, critic, André Suarès (1868–1948) is doubtless best known for his critical portraits of Pascal, Goethe, Tolstoy, and for his three volumes of Italian impressions, in which he depicts himself as a knight-errant of beauty wandering through Tuscany, Umbria, and Lombardy.

[8] The *N.R.F.* or *Nouvelle Revue Française,* a monthly literary periodical, was founded by André Gide and a group of friends in 1909. It continues today, although it suspended publication during the First World War and fell under German domination in the years 1940–4. Jacques Rivière was editor of the periodical from 1919 until his untimely death in 1925 at the age of thirty-nine.

and that all who wrote for the review had the most cordial attitude and often the keenest admiration for him, he had somehow got it into his head that I wanted to dominate there and was jealous of the consideration that was grudgingly granted him! It was only at the very end of his life that he finally became convinced that I not only did not hold a grudge for any of his fits of petulance, but held him in high esteem and suffered to see him so un-appreciated. For it is a fact that "criticism" in gen-eral and the young in particular made no effort to draw him out of the unsociable isolation into which he himself, through excess of pride, took a painful pleasure in letting himself sink. Yes, he suffered from *priditis* (this word that I invented for him fitted perfectly), from a deep-seated *priditis*. The wonderful portraits he had sketched in the past of Stendhal, of Tintoretto, of Joinville, of so many others, were unknown; but he was never satisfied until he had returned to the subject of himself, to the Condottiere he wanted to be, to Caërdal, to Suarès, unable to endure being lost sight of. A de-voted friend, Pierre de Massot, who knew both of us equally well though he was considerably younger, with utter tact, constant selflessness, and an understanding that came from the heart as

E

much as from the mind succeeded in sweeping
away the monsters that Suarès was wantonly keeping alive: he agreed to see me, to receive me. . . .
A certain letter that Massot showed me even revealed a desire to renew the relations he had unfortunately broken off with me. Then it was my
turn to dread that encounter. It seemed to me that,
even after he had seen the light, Suarès could not
forget (I was about to say: could not forgive me) a
certain article full of hatred and injustice that he
had not been able to keep himself from writing
recently against Chopin just after the publication
of my *Notes* in the *Revue Musicale*.[9] Is there any
need of saying that no one was better qualified
than Suarès to appreciate Chopin and to speak of
him with masterful authority? But he had not *discovered* Chopin. It was even evident in those few
vehement and rash pages he had just brought out
that he was barely familiar enough with Chopin to
provide a dubious substance for his violence. No

[9] Gide's *Notes on Chopin* first appeared in the *Revue Musicale* in December 1931, and Suarès's attack on Chopin came
out in the weekly *Nouvelles Littéraires* in March 1932. Under
date of 5 March 1932 in his *Journals*, Gide notes: "Suarès lets
his ignorance appear unwillingly. It becomes obvious, from
reading that article, that all he knows of Chopin is his waltzes,
polonaises, and mazurkas (together with the *Marche funè-
bre*)." He returns to the subject on 6 June 1933.

doubt he would have admitted his mistake as he once did with Dostoevsky, when he confessed to me that he had read only *Crime and Punishment* and *The House of the Dead* at the time I first spoke to him of the Russian writer. (I have related this somewhere or other.) [1] But it was too late; the monstrously unjust article had appeared, in which Suarès had given himself away. What a pity!

Before leaving the subject of Suarès, why not set down the recollection of that interminable evening we spent beside each other, when, all evening long, Suarès persistently kept his hand up against his face to screen it from my eyes. It was at the Cirque Médrano. Once a year I was accustomed to take Mme Allégret to the circus with her six children.[2] We took our seats in the front row, next to the arena. I was the last in the group. On my right the seat remained empty until there came to sit in it, to our mutual astonishment, Suarès. Oh, what a fine opportunity to recognize

[1] In his *Three Men* of 1913, Suarès claimed that he had not previously spoken of Dostoevsky because he was holding him in reserve. But Gide points out in his *Journals* for 11 December 1921 that Suarès based his essay on a hasty reading of the Russian novelist, for he had not read him earlier.

[2] Mme Elie Allégret was the wife of a Protestant minister whom Gide had known since childhood. Of her many children Gide eventually adopted Marc as his son.

51

each other! What! you too like the circus? Oh, but not so much as I . . . Yes, I do! That screening hand, forming a mystical, opaque wall. Even after the intermission, when we both returned to our seats. Had he deigned to look in my direction, I warrant that he would have encountered only a smile of the most kindly sort, or perhaps a downright laugh. It all struck me as comical. Decidedly, the only people I can take seriously are the unpretentious, and I can mingle spontaneously only with them. Buskins and high heels antagonize me. I am anxious to remain on the same footing.

At another evening (or matinee) at the Médrano I saw a swallower of goldfish and frogs. A very painful exhibition, and even more so because the wretched swallower seemed so ill-adapted to such a repulsive show. There was nothing of the mountebank about him. He looked rather like an "intellectual" reduced to that extremity by poverty. A handsome, contorted, and sorrowful face like Artaud's . . .[3] Now he is circling the arena, coughing up one after the other frogs and fish, the whole

---

[3] Antonin Artaud (1896–1948) was a Surrealist poet, actor, dramatist, and, above all, theorist of stagecraft. His emaciated face, deep-set eyes, broad forehead, and shock of unruly hair made him look like a tortured neurotic.

52

aquarium he had swallowed. I am sitting, according to custom, with the Allégret family in the front row. To my surprise, when he gets in front of me, the swallower, after having vomited a last frog, stops a moment, leans over, and says to *me* in a confessional whisper containing a suggestion of anguish: "What a man comes to do, nevertheless!!"

Did I fancy all that? Not the remark itself, to be sure (I can still hear it), but the anguish behind it? It may be; we never get very far into someone else's heart of hearts. We see and hear things, but everything below the surface remains a mystery. This is partly why in my *Faux-Monnayeurs*[4] I forbade myself, so to speak methodically, the current turns of phrase that novelists use: "He thought that . . ." "He could not believe that . . ." "He said to himself that . . ." What do you know about it, dear colleague? You want to impress us and no one will protest. Indeed, you can go so far as to seem exceptionally penetrating if you just add some reflection quite different from the common-sense

---

[4] In his logbook of the writing of *The Counterfeiters* (entitled *Journal of "The Counterfeiters"* and now published together with the novel), Gide discusses at length his fictional technique.

one we had a right to expect. For instance: "He said that without exactly thinking so" or "In his heart he did not doubt that . . ."

Consequently this is why I so often adopted the form of narration that made such subterfuges impossible, relating most of my tales in the first person. To be sure, in the "diary" (whether Alissa's, that of the minister in my *Symphonie pastorale*, of the uncle in my *Faux-Monnayeurs*, etc.[5] the sincerity can just as well be questioned, but the game is subtler and the reader is invited to take part in it. He is "in league" with the author. The dramatic form does not present such dangers. But whether in drama or in fiction, the best is to override this. A true creator must not even think of it. And that leaves room for unexpected strokes of genius, as revelatory as Balthazar Claës's exclamation to his wife (which Valéry admired so much): "The saints saved you" [6]—in which the unconscious and involuntary survival of his childhood

---

[5] Not only Alissa's diary in *Strait Is the Gate*, the Pastor's in *The Pastoral Symphony*, and the novelist's in *The Counterfeiters* are in the first person; *The Immoralist, Isabelle, The School for Wives*, and its two sequels also employ the same device.

[6] In Balzac's *Quest of the Absolute*, when a glass shield bursts in his wife's face without harming her, the hero exclaims: "God be praised! . . . The saints saved you from death!"

beliefs bursts forth despite the agnosticism contributed by his whole career as an atheist. But it may be regretted that such flashes are very rare in Balzac. (With Stendhal, a hint is enough for understanding.) Nothing could be more expected, more consistent than the remarks of Balzac's characters: most often they say just what you know in advance they are to say. They make me think of that hospital nurse in the shape of a hen represented in an American cartoon. She is opening the door of the delivery room to announce to the rooster (cigarette in his beak and his short wings behind his back in the manner of Napoleon, he is pacing up and down the waiting-room floor, which is strewn with cigarette butts) with an air of mystery the surprising news: "It's an egg." That cartoon delighted me. Too bad if you don't see the connection. . . .[7]

Nothing is less easy to transmit than laughter, or at least what provokes it. It is contagious, like yawning, but that's not at all the same thing. Nevertheless, I am very sensitive to the humor of

[7] I didn't see the cartoon. A friend, who saw it, tells me that I am wrong; it is not a chicken hospital, but a human hospital. Hence it is not a hen, but rather a human nurse who is announcing the news to the rooster. The joke still holds, though it changes character. [A.]

some of those stories the Americans call, I believe, "dog stories." [8] I can't resist giving a few examples of them. In a café a man and a dog are facing each other over a checkerboard. The dog pushes a checker with his paw. An individual approaches in amazement: "Why, your dog is really playing! He's remarkably intelligent . . ." Whereupon the man interrupts him: "Come now, don't exaggerate; he just lost the last two games."

Does that amuse you? Well, then, listen to this one: It takes place in a movie theater. A member of the audience sees a woman sitting in front of him and, to his amazement, a bear is in the seat next to her. The bear steps out during the intermission, and the man hastens to ask: "Excuse me, but can I believe my eyes? Is it a bear beside you?" "Why, of course, it's a bear." "Does he like the film?" "I don't know yet, but I can tell you that he liked the novel very much."

Or this one: Beside the pond in the Tuileries an individual throws a stick. His dog immediately rushes out on the surface of the water and brings it back to him. They repeat the game. Whereupon a bystander says in amazement: "Why, I say, your

[8] Although this is the term André Gide uses, he obviously means "shaggy-dog stories."

dog walks on the water!?" To which the man replies in the most natural tone of voice: "Of course! . . . doesn't know how to swim."

I know twenty more. I have tried to invent some myself. Just try. You will see that it's not so easy, although they all have the same character deriving from the same substitution of paradox for reality. How those stories take shape and are then transmitted is still something of a mystery to me. They remain anonymous and belong to a sort of folklore in which the genius of a race reveals itself, much more than the conscious work of an individual. Certain collections attempting to group them are quite disappointing and so badly put together that you wonder if the compiler himself is not an idiot. I had begun to set down the ones that seemed to me the juiciest in a notebook I entitled "Manual of the Complete Conversationalist." There were two parts to it: the collection of made-up stories followed the anthology of true remarks that it seemed to me a shame to let sink into oblivion. Moreover, the plan has not been altogether forsaken. . . .

Some of them seemed to you very good at first; some, born of circumstances, fade rather rapidly. But this one is still timely, though it used to circulate throughout the unsubjugated parts of Europe at the time of the first Moscow trials. Frontier guards were instructed to shoot at all those who tried to cross the line of demarcation into the free zone. One evening a certain guard, to his amazement, sees a great number of rabbits rush toward the line. "We beg you, let us pass!"—"But what's the matter with you boys?"—"Well, we have been told confidentially that soon all giraffes in the country will be wiped out." Leaning over toward them, the guard laughs as he says: "But, boys, you are certainly aware that you are not giraffes!"—"Yes," says the rabbit delegate, trembling with fright, "yes, of course . . . but how can we prove it?"

That story sent cold shivers down your spine. . . .

You hear them and you forget them. The best way to remember them is to repeat them at once, as I am doing with this one that I have just been told:

Dupont is traveling with Lévy. In the fast train to Paris, they both have berths. The train is to get in early, with just time enough to wash up before getting off. Dupont gets up first, spends the least possible time in the common washroom, then tells his unknown travelling-companion that he is free to go ahead. As soon as the latter has closed the door, he opens it again: "Excuse me, but I've already locked my suitcase; would you be kind enough to lend me your soap for a moment?" Dupont assents. The washroom door does not stay closed for long: "Would you allow me to use your comb for a minute?" Dupont lends his comb, but with a little less alacrity. And when Lévy, for the third time, opens the door and asks if Dupont would be kind enough to lend him his toothbrush too, Dupont bridles at last: "I'll go as far as the comb, but as for the toothbrush, no, really, forgive me. . . ." —"All right, all right, I won't insist. . . ."

When the train reaches Paris, everyone gets out. The following scene takes place at Lévy's. Mme Lévy asks her husband if his trip was all right. "Not bad," Lévy replies; "but there was an anti-Semite in my compartment. . . ."

I am relating as briefly as I can, but such stories are better when they are somewhat drawn out. . . . The toothbrush reminds me of the experience of my brother-in-law, Marcel Drouin,[9] who had

[9] Marcel Drouin (1870–1946) married Jeanne Rondeaux, the younger sister of Mme André Gide. He taught philosophy in *lycées* of Bordeaux, Alençon, and Paris and, under the pseudonym of Michel Arnauld, was an occasional essayist and critic. After a brilliant record at the Ecole Normale Supérieure and

undertaken to get a new one in the tiny village of Criquetot-L'Esneval, two kilometers from Cuverville, where we were spending a vacation period together. I had warned Marcel that he would come back empty-handed. When he gets back, I question him. In vain he had asked the pharmacist and the barber; perhaps the dry-goods store . . . The proprietress had questioned him at length, repeating: "*Une brosse à dents . . . à dents,* you say? But may I ask, Sir, for what purpose? . . ." The French *à* (see Littré) is used in so many expressions: *Un fer à friser, la mer à boire, une chance à courir, une chute à se casser les reins,* etc.[1] French, which seems so simple to us, is a very difficult language full of little pitfalls. I know foreigners who speak it wondrously well (*à merveille*) but who still stumble over the use of *si* with the indicative. I am ready to understand them; this is one of the anomalies of our language; the foreigner feels that *if* should be followed by the subjunctive, or at least the conditional.

There is perhaps no gift that I envy more than

---

sojourns in Germany, he helped Gide found the *Nouvelle Revue Française.*

[1] "a curling-iron," "impossible," "a risk worth taking," "a back-breaking fall." The proprietress of the shop took *brosse à dents* to mean "a brush with teeth."

the "gift of tongues," nor any that was more stingily meted out to me. Goethe was probably right in claiming that the fear of ridicule held back many French in this regard. Yet it is not so much fear of causing laughter that keeps me from using the little German, English, or Italian I know as it is a horror of boners, of . . . oh! yes, yes, Goethe is right: nonetheless and all the same, it is still a fear of ridicule.

I didn't apply myself to English until very late, but I did so resolutely, and wasn't satisfied until I could read with ease so many writers of all sorts who make of English literature the richest in the whole world. "I can't speak English" was for a long time the only sentence I could utter. I first had occasion to use it during the first and very short trip I made to London with our minister M. Allégret, to whom my mother had entrusted me.[2] He took me to hear a preacher named Spurgeon, famous then, who, after the sermon, used to baptize adults in an *ad hoc* pool. Dressed for the occasion in appropriate clothing (at least I hope so

[2] Elie Allégret, a Protestant minister, was André Gide's tutor and the best man at his wedding. He later became the director of all French Protestant Missions.

for them), they took part in a total immersion, which we watched. After the service, when everyone was leaving, a very seemly young lady came up to me at the door and said a few words in the sweetest voice, to which I smilingly protested: "No, thank you" (*that* I knew how to say), thinking that she was offering to do me some service or other. She immediately drew herself up, and from her hurt manner I suspected that that was not what I should have answered. M. Allégret had heard everything. "She was asking you if you wanted to be saved," he explained. The rest of the trip I prudently remained mute.

A big discussion about Molière arose spontaneously on the terrace at Cabris on the eve of my departure. I was the only one to defend Molière, though granting that he didn't "make me laugh" either. But I protested at once that it is far from being the comic element that delights me in Molière, but rather the style, outstanding among all others, the solidity, the substance in short, everything that by contrast gives a semblance of fragility, tenuousness, preciosity, and subtlety to other more charming products that are likely to captivate us at once. I floundered somewhat, discovering how hard it is to defend a writer, no matter how great, when his attacker begins by declaring himself insensitive to the fundamental virtues and disregards all that strikes him as antiquated. This is the way Léautaud is in regard to Racine, Breton in regard to La Fontaine, Roger Martin du Gard in regard to Balzac, etc.[3] Pointing to myself, I admitted that I had somehow been insensitive until recent years to the authority of Cervantes, for instance; yet that, though I now place him among the greatest, I still have to confess that he doesn't make me *laugh,* and that this doesn't matter to me at all and in no way decreases in my eyes his conspicuous qualities. Hence, in order to last, that work had to contain other virtues in addition to its *vis comica;* and I maintained that it just happened to be the same with Molière, Aristophanes, Plautus, and Rabelais. Here the conversation

---

[3] Paul Léautaud (1872–1956) was known for his unorthodox and outspoken opinions; his vast reputation as the fiery eccentric of his time really began with his series of radio interviews in 1950–1 and the subsequent publication of his *Literary Journal.* The high priest of Surrealism, André Breton (1896–   ), is also famous for his forthright judgments of the classics; but it is harder to understand why Roger Martin du Gard (1881–1958), the novelist of *The World of the Thibaults,* could not "endure" Balzac, as Gide noted in his *Journals* for 1928.

took a new turn, for, when I asked if one could be
sure that the irresistible humor of Charlie would
still cause laughter fifty years from now, H. argued
the necessity of distinguishing between types of
laughter, between what is intentionally provoked
and lasts but a time and what irresistibly accompanies a certain intellectual blind spot, a certain
odd behavior, or a certain exaggeration of pride.
The latter found a perfect example in Charlie. And
as others protested (there were five of us), it
finally dawned upon us that two of us were talking
of Charlie Du Bos while the three others were
thinking of Charlie Chaplin. It is often this way in
conversation: after a period of futile dispute, people notice that they were not talking of the same
thing. But often the same object seen in a different
light occasions the misunderstanding. One admired
Venice in bright sunlight, whereas I saw it only in
the rain. You have noted that *dubbing* spoils a film
that you were right to consider very remarkable in
its original version. Consequently this is why, oh!
conversations bore me! How I fear and flee them.
It is so rare that a person tries to understand someone else, or even to *hear* him! And what a waste of
strength and time if you agree, as I am first tempted
to do out of kindness. I struggle against that tend-

ency, and believe I am somewhat better able to resist than I once was. But it is so much simpler and less costly to approve! The trouble is that weeks, or months, or even years later, your interlocutor comes and reminds you: "But that's not at all what you told me in April 19 . . ."

Oh, to go back to the time when people were very little concerned as to my opinion about individuals, works, and things . . . which allowed me not to have any at all. Today America or China is eager, it seems, to know what I think about the atom bomb, the latest vote in the English Parliament, etc. I *ask* you! (A particularly difficult exclamation to translate.)

One of Jammes's stories that he told delightfully during his second stay at La Roque (during his first stay he talked only of the townsfolk of Orthez) [4] shook us with irrepressible laughter, for he told it with an incredibly droll accent: A disciple of Confucius came to ask him what he thought of death. Confucius replied that he thought nothing of it.

I am capable of indignation when faced with

[4] Francis Jammes (1868–1938), the pastoral poet of Orthez, visited Gide at his Norman estate of La Roque-Baignard in 1898.

certain abuses of force or injustices or cowardices, but most of the time what I witness arouses no desire for judgment, any more than the contemplation of a landscape, a plant, or an insect. Even though some human beings, I admit, are repulsive, I immediately turn my eyes toward those I can like and even, at times, consider admirable. The same is true for books, and often I take greater pleasure in rereading. So it is that I have just re-read, once more, the *Malade imaginaire* and the *Bourgeois gentilhomme* in order to convince myself once more after the discussion at Cabris that Molière "holds up," that he bears the attacks of time and of new fashions, that his work weathers well. And what a style! How his heels ring as they strike the ground! By contrast, Marivaux seems to walk on tiptoe. But don't go looking for any blame in these words. I like each of them as he is. Yet, for a Molière, I should give ten Marivaux.

Back in Paris, where life resumes its savor, I again take pleasure in living. What is the use of constantly reminding myself of my age? Let's leave that to infirmities. They bother me, to be sure, but none of them is unbearable. Hardly being able to

walk any more keeps me more at home. I shall try
to persuade myself that this is for the best.

If only others leave me alone! O bliss! . . . so
keen that I doubt whether I shall be able to sleep
tonight, and tomorrow I may feel as if laid flat
with sleeplessness. Indeed, it is essential for me not
to encounter my image in a mirror: those bags
under the eyes, those hollow cheeks, those drawn
features, those lackluster eyes. . . . I am enough
to frighten anyone, and that gives me a dreadful
fit of the blues. But let us carry on anyway. And to
think that I was an excellent walker, even runner.
I know very well the two or three times that I
strained my heart irremediably. The first was
cycling up a steep slope to join . . . The second,
through an acrobatic recovery of balance in a gar-
ret at Saint-Clair to join . . . Lastly and much
more recently, scaling rocks near the source of the
Adonis to join . . . So that, if I had a sudden heart
attack the next day in the plane, it was natural for
people to attribute it to the height; obviously; but
I knew that it was due especially and originally
to my rashness of the day before. To obtain what
I want I am tenacious, bold, even foolhardy, and
without a thought for the obstacles, but to resist

what puritans call "temptation" I am no good. I don't even try. If I believed in the devil (I sometimes pretended to believe in him; it's so convenient!), I should say that I come to terms with him at once.

In Paris I also find the familiar disorder and litter: not a table, not a shelf that is not overloaded with books. Books that I should not find time to read even if I did nothing but that, to read "I am not saying line by line but page by page" as Thadée N. wrote me so funnily about *Paludes,* which I had just sent him.[5] Every day the mail brings new ones. Some are accompanied by a letter. Other letters accompany manuscripts: the author needs to know what I think of his poems (most often what I am sent are verses). How disturbing such appeals can be! Not being aware of this is almost the only excuse for those who send them out. Most often I try to go ahead and not listen to them, not really hear them. Then I turn back to them. Nevertheless, supposing I were wrong! . . . Occasionally I was guilty of such crude, such unpardonable mistakes, with Proust, for instance, with Dorothy

---

[5] *Paludes* (*Marshlands*) of 1895 was Gide's first wholly ironic work. Thadée Natanson and his brother Alexandre had founded the *Revue Blanche* in 1891.

Bussy. . . .[6] Would I have recognized at once the extraordinary value of Baudelaire, of Rimbaud? Might I not at the outset have looked upon Lautréamont as a madman?[7] And eventually the question must be asked in the most serious way possible: am I capable of being moved by an utterly new form of poetry that breaks with tradition in every regard? And isn't that just what would deserve praise most of all? Even though it is not enough, as a proof of genius, to break with the artificial, the conventional, etc. . . .

---

[6] As principal reader for the *N.R.F.* publishing-house that grew out of his monthly periodical, Gide rejected the manuscript of Proust's *Swann's Way* in 1912 on a hasty reading. He recalled Proust only as a social butterfly of the nineties and was shocked by Proust's offer to subsidize the publication. But his contrite and admiring letters of January 1914 (when very few had yet appreciated the strange new novel) and his eventually successful efforts to acquire the rights from the original publisher and bring Proust under the *N.R.F.* imprint compensate for his mistake. Likewise, although Dorothy Bussy was an old friend and his English translator, Gide kept the manuscript of her novel *Olivia* for years because he thought it devoid of literary interest. When it was published in English and in French in 1949, it was an immediate success, however.

[7] Although Lautréamont's chief work, *Les Chants de Maldoror,* was first published as a whole in 1869, the year of Gide's birth, Gide first mentions enthusiastically a reading of the sixth canto in his *Journals* for November 1905. Before then, others had spoken of Lautréamont (Isidore Ducasse, 1846–1870) as a madman of genius, but Gide's enthusiasm long anticipated the glorification of Lautréamont by the Surrealists in the twenties.

Were I to find myself suddenly faced with a few new burning bushes comparable to the *Illuminations*, to the *Chants de Maldoror*, and supposing that I should recognize their radiance at once, I fear that at present I might be less dazzled than embarrassed by it. At my age, and for some time now, I have had my fill of poetry. The same is true for music; and I am almost on the point of adding: and for love. The young adventurer launching out into life fills his heart very readily, though there are many competing for the honor. And it is better thus. Dante may subsequently meet other Beatrices, Romeo other Juliets; he will not even glance at them, for he has his adequate supply of love and adoration. The rapture and enthusiasm that Hugo inspired in me when I read him at sixteen may be kindled in the heart of to-day's adolescents by others than Hugo. Each of us feels a special gratitude to the one who initiated him. And nothing subsequently can equal those initial raptures.

But it also occurs, both for love and for admiration, that the most solid attachments are the tardy ones.

In Paris I must resign myself to the disorder and the clutter that result. But what a mistake it would be to think that I like that disorder! Occasionally I get to the point of not being able to find a place to write. And what an effort I must deliberately make to abstract myself, not to see what attracts my mind in so many different directions! But if I began to try to put in order the books and papers that have piled up almost at random, it would take me hours and days. I give up; it is easier to pack one's bag and get away anywhere. How often have I started on a trip merely to get away from Paris! And yet Paris is the place where the intellectual ferment is the most intense. But the fatigue too. After a short time I am worn out; I get away.

Moreover, I don't really need to be settled down to get to work. I write anywhere whatever, on a café table, on a boulevard bench, in a moving train. . . . During this long automobile trip back to Paris, I twice asked Gilbert, my chauffeur, to stop so that I could write down what I feared not to remember at the next regular stop—and which I set down here:

In my testamentary arrangements I left no direction regarding my funeral and am worried about the situation my executors will be in. But, however

I sound myself out, I cannot get myself to make a definite decision. Cremation, to tell the truth, does not seem unattractive. I am rather tempted by it, but I confess that I prefer being nibbled by worms and absorbed by the roots of plants and trees to being sniffed haphazardly by a lot of halitosis-ridden jean-foutre *(what-the-hell-do-I-care's).*

I am somewhat embarrassed by *"jean-foutre"* and don't know how to put it in the plural. In vain I look in the Littré for that very handsome nasty expression, whose origin I should like to know, and in the most instructive *Courrier de Vaugelas* which I have had bound in two thick volumes.[8] Furthermore, in setting down that sentence that I originally liked, I detect in it a rather aggressive cynicism that is not at all like me.

How beautiful "Napoleon's route" via Saint-Vallier and Grenoble seemed to me! I was taking it for the first time. Yet I cursed the roof of my car, which cut me off from nature and allowed me to see only bits of the landscape. I like open cars,

---

[8] The *Courrier de Vaugelas* was a periodical published in ten thin volumes by Eman Martin between 1868 and 1887 for "the universal propagation of the French language." It took its title from the fascinating *Remarques* (1647) of the grammarian Claude Favre de Vaugelas (1585–1650).

even though, as I am assured, they no longer suit my age.[9] But what a pleasure! And then, to force a sudden stop when I see an unknown plant by the roadside, I can give a flick to my hat that will send it flying. In the U.S.S.R. I recall that it took a certain courage to employ the hat trick and force our Rolls Royce to stop. It was during a wonderful excursion in the Caucasus. What *was* that dazzlingly red isolated flower at some little distance from the road toward which I ran through the fields while some zealous companions went after my headgear? But it was merely a quite common poppy just like all the poppies in France. Set off alone in that field, it seemed a marvel. . . .

I detest funerals, and repeat to myself Christ's words: "Let the dead bury their dead" every time that, out of a sense of propriety, I think I am obliged to take part in one of those funeral ceremonies at which a very few cases of sincere sorrow are aped by a large number of counterfeiters. And all those hands to shake! after which one feels

---

[9] When a friend of mine, the painter Cécile Bellé, met André Gide in June 1948, he questioned her about American makes of cars. Obviously he had decided on a convertible, but she pointed out to him that an open car was hardly the thing for someone who wore a beret even in his own apartment in June.

an urgent need to wash one's own . . . I prefer
to decline, making an exception only for the cases
in which my absence might be interpreted as
scorn or coldness. For twenty years I have kept in
my wallet this card from the sister of a char-
woman for whom I had a deep attachment. The
card comes from "Mademoiselle Vieillard" (San-
tenay, Côte d'Or) and reads:

DEAR SIR:
*Crushed with sorrow, I want to inform you of
the dreadful news: my dear sister Eugénie passed
away last night. She had got up after a fit of chok-
ing. The doctor came at once, but his efforts were
useless. I can't believe it; she so full of life just
yesterday!* . . .

Poor good woman, so devoted, so sensitive, so
thin! . . . I can still see her; I can still hear her,
one day as she was busy in Marc Allégret's study,
next to mine, when he lost patience over the tele-
phone to the point of letting fly a most unac-
customed oath, *"bordel de Dieu";* [1] whereupon
Eugénie, generally so reserved, interrupting her
sweeping a moment, exclaimed: "Why, that's

----

[1] "God's brothel" is the literal meaning of this unusual oath.

odd . . . precisely my late father's favorite oath!"
(Let me add in haste that she was most pious.) It
had never occurred to me until then that Eugénie
Vieillard had had a father.

Mme Théo has given me her beret to take the
place of a little travelling-hat that I always had
with me but most often carried folded up under
my arm. She assured me that it had served long
enough and had become unwearable. True, it did
draw attention to itself, and to me under it; and it
was rather ridiculous. I had bought it at Karlovy-
Vary, which at that time was still called Karlsbad,
where I had gone to take the cure for I don't remember just which ailment. The first time I went
out into the town, I stopped dead in front of a hat
shop, or, more specifically, in front of a jaunty little
hat of which I had never seen the like. It was as
soft as anyone could want (I don't like hats to be
stiff), light in weight, and pleasantly coffee-col-
ored; in short, I bought it at once. But as I continued my walk I didn't meet a soul who was not
bareheaded. So that, back in the hotel, I consigned
my acquisition to a shelf, waiting to sport it until
I should get back to France. This took place in the
morning. Now, I found out that an exceptional

75

ceremony was going to take place in a synagogue,
and that I shouldn't miss hearing a famous chorus
of Jewish singers. I hastened there, but was stopped
at the door, for no one could enter without a hat.
But I was told at once that the porter rented hats
to uninformed outsiders. The indispensable headgear that the porter offered me was a sort of bat-
tered top hat, so filthy that I hated to put it on.
Throughout the whole ceremony I held it with
both hands an inch or so above my bald head,
while thinking of the jaunty little new hat waiting
on my shelf.[2]

What I am telling is not very interesting. I know
that, yet I am writing it anyway, just as simply as
I should tell it to you if you were sitting here beside me and each of us smoking a cigarette. I
should so much like you not to feel any distance between us and to think: I didn't need him to indulge
in such a thought . . . hence, of course, I am led
to bring forth a few platitudes.

The younger of my sisters-in-law used to excel
in what she called "Chinese proverbs."[3] I don't

---

[2] André Gide had already told this story in his *Journals* under the date of 22 July 1934.

[3] Valentine Rondeaux (1870–?), the youngest sister of
Madeleine Rondeaux (Gide), who married Marcel Gilbert and
lived in Pau.

know where she may have got them, but they always came in appropriately in a discussion when she thought she was about to be at a disadvantage. It was often rather irritating, especially when one began to realize that she was inventing those proverbs *ad lib. "One cannot be angry with someone who makes a mistake with the best of intentions,* as a Chinese proverb states," she would say in the same tone of voice that, when somewhat younger, she had used to beat a retreat with a condescending "let's admit" that had made me wild. Or again: *Nothing gives greater assurance than error.*

Even as a child, she had an extraordinary sense of mystery. Her two sisters and I had it too, but it was less pronounced with us. For instance, when we were altogether "among ourselves" and talking about anything at all, Valentine would suddenly add to any ordinary remark what she called her "magic formula." I should have so much liked to know it. "Please, Valentine, say it very slowly once so that I can remember it."—"It has no value when it's not said rapidly. Still, I want to be nice, so I'll repeat it once more, but no more than once." And I could barely make out in a sort of mumble something like "Hossalaps allalip derfous."

Then there was this too, which seems to me much odder even today. Of my uncle's five children, the two considerably younger boys did not generally take part in our games, and I don't recall that they participated in the little ceremony I am about to describe, which even I witnessed but a single time. It all took place on the roof of a washhouse adjoining the kitchen, both of which were on the ground floor. That roof was boxed in except on top. It could be reached through a low door. It was like a little inner courtyard surrounded by high walls and sheltered from indiscreet eyes. I believe I had never set foot there; I am even ready to believe that I was unaware of its existence until the day when I was initiated to it.

I have said that my two boy cousins did not share in our games. In the light of that, I don't fully understand, for, after all, there had to be more than four to play "Signora Velcha." But I suddenly recall, or at least seem to recall, that Marguerite Waddington joined our procession. And indeed I wonder now if it was not she who had taught us the game. There must have been a tradition, for everything took place according to a fixed rite. My three girl cousins and Miss Waddington, Valentine's friend, had covered their faces

with a sort of dust-sheet; in Indian file and progressing very slowly with measured step, circling
the little courtyard; and when the next to the last
in the procession passed the first (it was all regu-
lated like a ballet), they both raised their sheets,
stepped one step toward each other and said in
a deep voice and most seriously, each speaking to
the other but timing it so they spoke simultaneously, the following words: "Signora Velcha,
have you almost finished?" which called for no
reply. There would follow several moments of
anguished silence; then the procession would resume its circular march until the last one would
come abreast of the second one and the formula
would be repeated. "I'm too much afraid of making a mistake. No, leave me alone! I'll never be
able to play your game," I first screamed as I strug-
gled. Valentine insisted: "Yes, yes, you must know.
It is time for you to learn." Valentine was rather
proud of her relationship with Marguerite Waddington, whose father was or had been an ambas-
sador. I can still see her—beautiful, perhaps
rather scornful or haughty, and probably already
possessing all the qualities that subsequently allowed her to become the head (isn't Mother Superior the title?) of the convent of Vanves, where

79

Jacques Copeau's second daughter took the veil.[4] In Madagascar now, the latter still prays for her parents' old friend, who loved her dearly.

Agnès Copeau was my wife's best friend. The Copeau family in its entirety had accepted our invitation to come to Cuverville and share with us the anxiety occasioned by the outbreak of war. At that time Edi Copeau, the future nun, was still in the cradle. She was charming. On her little forehead her blond hair stood up like points, despite cosmetics. I used to call her *Igel,* which in another language meant "porcupine." Meanwhile Jacques was working on *The Brothers Karamazov.*[5]

But perhaps I am wrong (I should never be trusted for dates). Wasn't it rather on *La Maison natale* that he was working then?[6] And did not the adaptation of Dostoevsky's masterpiece form the joyous torment of another stay with us?

[4] Edi (Edwige) Copeau, the second daughter of Gide's associate Jacques Copeau and of Madeleine Gide's close friend Agnès Copeau, entered the Order of Benedictine Missionaries in 1931 at Vanves with the name of Mère François; she has since been stationed in Madagascar.

[5] The stage adaptation that Jacques Copeau and Jean Croué made of *The Brothers Karamazov* was first produced in 1911.

[6] In fact, it was in June 1914 that Copeau was working at Cuverville on his only original full-length play, *La Maison natale* (*The Family Home*), which he produced at his own theater in 1923.

Everything is getting confused in my heart and head. And, particularly in my dreams, I witness dumbfounding superimpressions and get to the point of not knowing at all where I stand. From the practical point of view, this can become most embarrassing; as, for instance, to confuse the characters of a play or a film or of life and to mistake one for another. And, furthermore, this only encourages excessively a certain natural suspicion with regard to what we are obliged to call reality —of which I have spoken overabundantly elsewhere.[7]

When I was very young, I often had occasion to launch out at night into dreadful nightmares from which I would come forth trembling and bathed in tears. Later, I don't know what took place in my organism, nor what endocrine glands had begun to function differently, but the feeling of fear left me. I still dreamed of the same bugaboos, but without taking them seriously; I could still be gobbled up by the goblin, but it all seemed a joke to me. In so-called real life I am most often pru-

---

[7] Frequently in his *Journals* Gide alludes to his lack of "the *feeling of reality*" (20 December 1924), his "disbelief in reality" (28 July 1929), and the fact that his "*reality* always remains slightly fantastic" (23 June 1930).

dent and cautious; but at times the demon of curiosity carries the day (I should say "carries me away") and makes me careless of danger. Like that night when, very late, I had ventured onto the stairs of the Algiers harbor in pursuit of two young Arabs who seemed to me very strange. A very well-dressed gentleman—and certainly with a charitable intention—whispered in a quite distinct and quite distinguished voice (we were still on the upper quay, but it was obvious that I was on the point of going down toward the ill-lighted docks) as I passed near him (but what was he himself doing on that deserted quay?): "Watch out, Sir; what you are doing is extremely dangerous." I think I said "Thank you" to him as I raised my hat and lowered an embarrassed face. But when I raised my face the two boys had disappeared. And perhaps, after all, that stranger saved my life.

Another night, instead of two kids, it was two strapping fellows. . . . It was in Venice. On the Riva degli Schiavoni I had got into their gondola with no sinister intention. You may be sure that if I had had sinister intentions, I should make no bones about telling you. No, I was thinking only of spending an hour in a gondola before going to bed prudently; otherwise, I should have begun by choosing other gondoliers than these two stalwarts, who were no longer very young. Hence, I had stretched out in the bottom of the gondola without seeing anything but the sky above my head. At most I was aware that they were going up the Grand Canal; then I slipped into a carefree and poetic torpor. Suddenly the gondola stopped. What was going on? Where are we? Certainly not in the Grand Canal any more. From my recumbent position I had just had time to sit up in order to see one of my stalwarts standing in front of me between my legs and saying in a voice that was far from affectionate: *"Adesso, pagare."* From this I realized that he was inviting me to take out my wallet at once. With apparent innocence I managed to notice in a glance that the narrow canal we had entered flowed between deaf and blind walls, utterly inattentive and indifferent to whatever might go on at their base. I had no pistol on me (I never have) and no other weapon but a heavy stick, on which I leaned, so to speak, without changing position in the least. I realized (one suddenly becomes very intelligent in such cases) that the slightest move might be my undoing, or, more precisely, that I was lost if I let the slightest fear be seen, the least attempt at protection of myself or

83

the few banknotes I was carrying. Only one thing to do, I thought, and that is brazen it out. My apparent indifference saved me. Had I reached for my wallet, nothing would have been easier than to flick it out of my hand. Nothing was easier, after that, than to stun me by hitting me with the oar, to pitch me overboard, and subsequently nothing would be heard of me. As for dying by drowning, may I add, I should prefer other waters than the fetid and putrid waters of the Venetian canals.

The fellow was waiting, obviously surprised by my calmness. He repeated, but a little less imperatively: *"Adesso, pagare."* We stared at each other. *"Niente da fare,"* I said. Unfortunately, I didn't know Italian well enough to explain to him my firm intention of not paying him until he had taken me back to the Riva degli Schiavoni. I had to be satisfied with pronouncing the name of the quay, the same one where I had got into their gondola. He understood. I saw him shift from one foot to the other for a few moments as he hesitated. . . . When he had sat down again beside his companion, I offered each of them a cigarette that they laughingly accepted. The whole thing had amused me extraordinarily.

As to fear, it was in Ravenna that I made its acquaintance, utterly unreasoning and unreasonable. At the Hotel Byron we had a huge room with two beds. French windows opened directly onto a broad terrace, prolonged on a slightly lower level by the hotel garden. I have no idea whether all that still exists today. I have never gone back to Ravenna since that period of our wedding trip.[8] Each of the beds, although far removed from each other, faced the large French window, which we had left wide open because of the mildness of the weather. The light of the full moon filled half of the room. If I did not give these details, it would be impossible to understand what I am about to tell. Around midnight I was wakened by my wife's call; she asked me to get up and go and close the French window. It seemed to me that her voice was trembling. I had propped against my bed the same cane that had given me assurance against the gondoliers. I didn't let my wife see that I seized it at once. The empty space to cover before reaching the window seemed to me tremendous; for a few moments I doubted that I should have the strength and courage to cross it. As I returned to my bed immediately thereafter, I had but one

---

[8] The wedding trip took place in 1895–6.

concern: not to let my wife see that my knees were knocking together, and especially not to let her hear my teeth chatter; but wasn't this from fever even more than from fear? This is what I wondered only later on, remembering that we had spent the hottest hours of the day in an open carriage wandering over the fantastic swamps that surround the town, or that at least surrounded it then, famous for the malaria of which we were both feeling the effects.

It is only with great difficulty, and very rarely, that I manage to be the same age every day. Even as a child, my uncles and aunts used to call me "erratic." Can you understand the situation of someone who, in the course of a single day, could at one moment have at hand a considerable income and at another feel reduced almost to begging? How can one dare to make commitments when doubting whether one will be able to keep them? Lack of self-confidence can become paralyzing. Being unable to count on oneself. Will he who keeps the appointment be the same as he who made it? Whence my withdrawals, my escapes, my flights, my apparent inconstancy. It is bad enough not to recognize others; but what a nuisance it is not to recognize oneself! Hence let me withdraw from the game, for fear of letting you down. To-day I'll be glad to talk to you; tomorrow I may not have anything to say to you. . . .

Another thing hampers me too: not knowing how much credit I have in the minds of others. I wonder at and envy those naturally conceited people who rely on the conviction that everything is due them. What assurance that gives their bearing! When I put myself forward, I do so timorously; and most often I prefer not to put myself forward at all. That comes in part from the long habit of not being listened to at all. Therefore, it is better to keep silent. Whence comes perhaps the value, if it may be said to have any, of my *Journal;* with it I got even; in it I took refuge. Now that I know and feel in advance that people will give attention to what I am about to say, I have much less desire to speak. Yet, at times I am seized with a desire to place an anecdote. This is generally when the conversation lags, for I don't like silences. Now I dare launch out. Yet I don't have to go very far back to when I had but a single concern—that of reaching the end of the story rapidly for fear of not being allowed to finish it. So often I had been interrupted! Consequently I gallop. But, bang! the story is interrupted just "at the grandest moment," as Yvette Guilbert used to sing. And so often I tasted the mortification of having no one ask for the rest or utter a reassuring and comforting "And so? . . ." People begin talking of other things, and I have had all my trouble for nothing and once again have to tell myself: it would be better not to have begun than to be unable to finish.

Generally, conversations bore me, wear me out. Those with whom one can be natural are so rare! The moments spent conversing with those few are all the more charming and precious. I spoke of avarice, a while back: the thing I am least prodigal of is my time. I am angry with those who make me waste it and cannot convince myself that they take real pleasure in my company when I take so little in theirs. But during my youth it was not the same, to be sure; and at the time of the *Ermitage* and especially in the early years of the *Nouvelle Revue Française*, conversations were at their height: it was essential to be informed, to understand fully what we wanted and who we were; conversing was tantamount to collaborating, and our talks always had a purpose.[9] The book that

---

[9] At the height of its influence, from 1897 to 1906 under the editorship of Edouard Ducoté, *L'Ermitage* counted among its

Ghéon entitled *Nos Directions* reflects our end-
less discussions and stores up the results of our
efforts to lift literature and the arts out of the mud
and get them out of their rut.[1] Those who came
after us, not fully aware of how they had benefited
from the new direction we had indicated, soon lost
sight of the sorry state of "French letters" at that
time and of what a jerk we had had to give the
rudder to get the wagon out of the bog and back
on its course. (A plague on metaphors! This reminds one irresistibly of "the Ship of State traveling down the road, etc." Too bad, but . . .)

Let me go still farther back, to the period of
"Signora Velcha, have you almost finished?" to
mention another game that my cousins and I had
only too rarely a chance to play. It could only

regular contributors Claudel, Copeau, Ghéon, Gide, and Gour-
mont. In the early years of the *N.R.F.* (chiefly 1909–13)
everything was handled by a group of close friends; as one of
them, Jean Schlumberger says, "we wanted to talk of a thousand things that had no place in a book, to discuss freely all
the problems related to literature and its contacts with life."

[1] One of the first books to be published by the young *N.R.F.*
publishing-house, *Our Directions* (1911) contained a series of
essays on classicism, on rhythm, and on a poetic renaissance in
the theater. Ghéon states in it that the major question for him
and his friends is that of a dynamic equilibrium between matter and form, art and life, tradition and innovation.

have been in Rouen following certain family din-
ners at the Henri Rondeaux' in rue de Crosne.[2]
We, the children, were allowed to leave the table
immediately after dessert while the grownups
stayed on in the dining-room. All four of us would
then go to the drawing-room and, with a great
effort of memory, try to retrace the steps in the
conversation. We knew the point it had reached
at the moment when we left it. We also knew its
starting-point. Between these terminal points we
had to trace a sinuous line, full of meanders and
tangents, broken by interferences and more or less
fortuitous interruptions. It was an intellectual
game in which we were not always able to fill in
the gaps and uncertainties. "No, Aunt Lucile didn't
begin to complain of the strike at Le Houlme until
later, after Uncle Henri had pointed out that
strikes are as bad for employees as for employers."
"No, uncle's remark didn't come in until after that."

I used to like that game. I liked all gratuitous,
non-boisterous games. I recall that, much later,
when he became acquainted with the beginning
of *Si le grain ne meurt* . . . , Charlie Du Bos

---

[2] When André Gide and his mother would visit her native
Rouen, they usually stayed in the large house in rue de Crosne
belonging to her brother Henri Rondeaux.

made no effort to hide the fact that he was bored by the descriptions of the kaleidoscope, the marbles, and all I tell—probably at too great extent, I agree—about the diversions of my early childhood. He added: "Sorry, my dear Gide, *I* never played." And this allowed him to look with great severity on the play of others! But even today I doubt that such ignorance is a proof of superiority, whatever Pascal thinks.[3]

That my memory is not (at least, not always) trustworthy, I am well aware. Dominique Drouin, my nephew and godchild, has just contributed a new proof of this, so strange that I want to set it down here. And after that it will be readily understood why I hesitate to venture among the shifting sands of the past.

I am thinking of a tale he told me on returning from the First World War, in which Paul Gide, another nephew, had lost his life.[4] Domi himself had come out alive only by a miracle. The tale to

---

[3] One of Pascal's *Pensées* states: "The only thing that consoles us for our woes is entertainment, and yet it is the greatest of our woes."

[4] Paul Gide, the son of the economist Charles Gide, was actually André Gide's cousin, though much younger than he. Dominique Drouin is the son of Gide's brother-in-law, Marcel Drouin.

which I am alluding had impressed me so much that I had noted it in my *Journal*. I didn't even recall having noted it down; but apparently I recorded it so inaccurately that, quite recently, Domi felt obliged to bring it up. Nothing, absolutely nothing, of what I had said was accurate. I was shocked.

To make myself clear, let me set down first the few lines that are incriminated (*Journal* for the 15th of September 1931): "I think of that little soldier whom Domi saw die beside him in the ditch where they had both huddled. Less well sheltered than Domi, he got all the bullets. Domi heard them penetrate that tender flesh. And the little fellow (almost a child, Domi said) did not moan, but simply said, at moments, when he got a new wound: 'It's too much! Oh! it's too much! . . .' in a low voice, as if he were quite ready to suffer, but not that much."

"With what bursts of laughter," Domi told me, "I reread those lines a few days ago—that is, thirty years after the event—to André Desfeuilles, who knew very well the fellow in question. To begin with, he didn't die; less than six months later he was in perfect health. 'Almost a child,' you say.

. . . He was a big husky chap who thought only of having a good time . . . and so forth and so on. . . ." And Domi added, laughing himself: "I am not questioning (please don't misunderstand me) the sincerity with which . . . you invented the whole thing."

I reflected considerably about the question, with consternation in the beginning. But then my skepticism shifted gradually: "Invented the whole thing?" I am not so sure. Not at all sure now of not having telescoped two stories. For, after all, Domi's original account stirred me deeply; I'll even go so far as to say that my esteem and affection for Domi had been greatly increased as a result of that very account. For, in any case, what I had not been able to invent was my emotion. . . . It is nonetheless true that the recollection of an event can be (or become) quite different from the event itself and, so to speak, take its place. Children should be trained early and taught to bear witness without distortion. That ought to be part of a planned upbringing. Once a week, if I were a teacher, I should take my class into the street. A little accident would be all ready for the children to see, and then they would have to relate it simply.

The best "bystander" [5] would get the best grade
for a feat of reporting that would take the place of
his "French composition." A sort of emulation
would grow up, and the winner would be the one
who had managed to show the greatest objective
accuracy in his account.

My wife and I had seen the young king of Spain's
arrival in Paris.[6] All along the course his car took,
the streets were lined with people; we were in the
first row, so that it cannot be argued that we
didn't see him *clearly*. Then how can it be explained that, that very evening, talking over the
ceremony that had stirred us, we suddenly realized
with amazement that my wife had seen the young
king in a white uniform whereas he had appeared
to me in red? . . . Which of us was wrong? Impossible to find out: the newspapers did not
mention the color of his costume.

Yes, the effort of the earliest training should tend
to *desubjectivize* the child, to teach him to see and
feel things as they are in reality, to judge them independently of his personal reactions. Let me explain myself: At the family table at Cuverville the

[5] "Bystander" appears in English in the text.
[6] This visit of the young Alfonso XIII took place in May 1905.

94

same comedy is repeated every day: as soon as one asserts that it is very hot, that he is stifling, another protests that it so happens that that particular morning he is shivering. I protest in turn: "It matters little to me what you feel. I should like the children at this table to become capable of judging accurately the number of degrees the thermometer shows. It is essential to train them to do so, and this will cut short discussions. It doesn't take long to become quite expert in such a verifiable estimate. And that is much better than to overdress or underdress the children, as if trying to catch a cold, according to the prompting of purely subjective impressions." Whereupon my sister-in-law declares that she doesn't need a thermometer to know how to clothe her children and that her maternal instinct has never deceived her yet, whereas one always has to interpret the thermometer's readings. . . . And this would be the beginning of disputes in which we would get lost as in the deepest woods. One of the interlocutors then shouts "the woods" to imply that we'll never get out. Then quiet suddenly settles on us, as inexplicably as in those vespertine concerts of frogs there are sudden silences when all cease croaking at once by what seems a common agreement, just as all had begun to croak simultaneously. But let's not tarry on this.

I should like now to reveal some of my devices for guiding the choice of a secretary, male or female. It is essential not to commit oneself lightly. I know almost nothing about the girl who comes, and should like to put her to the test without her suspecting it. So this is what I think up. Expecting her visit, I have taken care to remove from my shelves a dozen volumes of Sainte-Beuve and to leave them scattered over the floor. "Miss (or Mrs. or Mr. followed by the name), please be so kind, while I am finishing a letter, as to put back on that shelf (to which I point) those books on the floor." And I leave her all the time necessary to perform that little task while I pretend to be absorbed in the letter that she sees me writing. All right. My letter and the tidying up are both finished. Then I get up to look at the Sainte-Beuves. Horrors! The *Lundis, Nouveaux Lundis, Portraits contemporains* etc., are all mixed up. Or else a Volume II is out of place after Volume X. Or else one of them (the volumes are bound) is upside down. "You should have told me that I was to put them in order."

"Miss, that was self-evident. Your sense of order is the one thing that will allow me to dispense with such a thing."

I remember the one who . . . I kept her three days. She was charming. It was not a sense of order, but intelligence, that she lacked. The evening of the third day, she told me that she had accomplished much: she had put order into my correspondence with Jammes.[7] I must first say that at that time neither of us dated his letters. Consequently I had taken great care to save the proper envelope with each letter, as the postmark sufficed to establish the date. She had made a thick packet of the revelatory envelopes, thus forever removing any way of getting one's bearings. As a result of that, I had gone on a trip without any secretary at all.

Those lapses of memory, even if my salvation were at stake . . . there is nothing to be done about them. There is something I once knew, and now, in place of the recollection, there is merely a great gap, white or black. The anecdote I am about to tell, which I have kept to myself until now, still

---

[7] The whole of the Gide-Jammes correspondence extending over a period of forty-five years was eventually edited by Robert Mallet, who found great difficulty in dating the letters.

wrings my heart today. But I cannot relate it without commenting on it. It concerns that weakness I was talking about.

Our trip in the U.S.S.R. was approaching its end.[8] Already Schiffrin and Guilloux had left us, the latter unable to endure a longer exile from home. Pierre Herbart, Jef Last, Dabit, and I were still holding up, and should have held up much longer—still interested, indeed more and more interested, by the strangeness of an exceptionally wonderful country and charmed by the warm cordiality of the inhabitants, which never once failed us. Subsequently there was talk of disappointments on our part, but nothing of the sort was true. At first contact a human communion existed with those whose language we couldn't speak—at least Dabit and I couldn't. As for Jef, within a week he was capable of understanding any speech whatever and within a fortnight of conversing; as for Pierre Herbart, he had just spent more than a year in Moscow. But that day, I don't recall why, Dabit

---

[8] In the summer of 1936 Gide spent two months in the Soviet Union as a guest of the Association of Soviet Writers. He took along five younger companions: the novelists Eugène Dabit and Louis Guilloux, both of humble birth; the Russian-born publisher Jacques Schiffrin; the journalist Pierre Herbart; and the Dutch writer Jef Last.

and I had remained alone in Sebastopol and had agreed to let a luxurious auto take us on a long excursion to one of the most modern youth camps, which surpassed anything we could have expected. That establishment, where we spent considerable time, is one of those of which the U.S.S.R. had most reason to be proud; the only trouble was that she boasted a little too much of it and that the children who benefited from those amazing advantages were kept in too dark an ignorance of the rest of the universe. But what I want to tell concerns the trip out, before Dabit felt the first signs of that scarlet fever which, a few days later, was to carry him off. Here the two of us are, then, stretched out in the back seat of the car, and never had Dabit been more charming or more inclined to reveal himself. He told me feelingly, almost sadly, of a certain pilgrimage he had made in the past to Cuverville. And I expressed amazement and asked for details. He had stood a long time contemplating that old family house, from which I was absent at the time. Discretion had kept him from entering the garden, where some of my nephews or nieces were playing. A fine rain had begun to fall, which still did not drive him away. He had followed the grove of beeches, recognized the little garden gate behind which my Alissa unexpectedly finds her Jérôme in *La Porte étroite,* had sat on the little bench at the end of the avenue of trees where Alissa says farewell to Jérôme and to the world, and at last had left, his heart brimming with tears and love. As he spoke, he had seized my hand, which he squeezed in his. And I listened to his account, shaken by his friendly enthusiasm. Since his first letter we had met many times, but without ever alluding to his visit to Cuverville. Hence I listened to his tale with surprise and emotion. His visit to Cuverville went back to June 1928, and it was now August 1936. He did not say: but I told you all this in the past. And the fact is that when, back in Paris, I looked up Dabit's letters, which I had carefully saved, I found the one of 4 June 1928 in which he relates that visit to the correspondent he still called "Monsieur Gide" in a way that still seems to me most moving—just as the apparent indifference with which I received that mark of youthful enthusiasm seems to me dreadful. I had no recollection whatsoever of it. What interpretation could he give to such a shameful forgetting? Scorn, coldness, or some other motive; but how can I doubt that he must have suffered from it?

The very evening of that day, he had to take to his bed. A doctor, called in haste, forbade anyone to enter his room, for fear of contagion. Through the open door I could still wave to him from a distance. And that was all. Three days later Pierre Herbart, Jef Last, and I returned to Moscow, where Dabit was to join us at any moment, after his temporary indisposition. On arriving in Moscow we found a sad telegram telling us of his death. It left us heartbroken. It would be impossible to imagine anyone more worthy of affection than Dabit.

As for the last days, the last hours of Dabit, surrounded by people who didn't speak his language and whose language he couldn't understand, I cannot think of them without horror. What must have been his anguish from the moment when he felt hopelessly lost, without recourse to anyone and with no possibility of calling for help. . . . We had left him only because of the near-certainty that he was passing through a momentary indisposition; but, in his eyes, didn't it seem as if we had forsaken him?

I reread his letters: profuse, diffuse, but from the very first ones of 1927 brimming with an excessive affection that actually frightened me somewhat.

Dabit asked of me not only a friendship that I most cordially granted him, but also literary guidance that would have required of me an expenditure of time that I didn't have free. He wanted me to read and help him to polish a long manuscript that he wanted to submit to me. Furthermore, I didn't feel especially qualified for that type of help. I thought of Roger Martin du Gard, perhaps a little freer than I, whose aesthetic was closer to Dabit's.[9] I took the liberty of bringing them together, and between them began a regular correspondence which made it possible for *Hôtel du Nord* to take form and become the very fine book that we now know. Only those who do not know the scrupulous attention of the author of *Les Thibault,* his professional conscience, and his abnegation in the cause of friendship, will express surprise at the great amount of time he devoted to that master-disciple guidance, which lasted I don't know how many months and years. I have no doubt of the excellence of the advice he constantly gave Dabit,

---

[9] Excessively modest and lacking in self-confidence at the beginning of his career, Eugène Dabit (1898–1936) needed the advice and attention he found in Roger Martin du Gard (1881–1958). Like the author of *The World of the Thibaults,* he patiently rewrote every page several times. Recognition came in 1929 with his first novel, *Hôtel du Nord.*

and believe that, should their exchange of letters come to be published someday, many other novices will find guidance and advantage in it. But the friendship Dabit felt for me was no less keen, and I was able to show him what I felt for him by inviting him to accompany me to Russia nine years later, with Guilloux, Schiffrin, Herbart, and Jef Last.

I gave but an inadequate glimpse of that trip in my *Retour de l'U.R.S.S.*[1] I regret not having noted down from day to day everything we had a chance to see and experience. But the constant surveillance to which I felt subjected and the fear of being taken indiscreetly by surprise kept me from putting into writing anything that might subsequently serve some perfidious purpose or other. But, since I am bringing those recollections up to the surface of my memory, let me take this occasion to protest once more against the rumor that spread, after the publication of my book, that the trip had disappointed me. Disappointed as to the total realization of Communism, of course; and what I said of this, as of the lack of individual liberty, understates the case. The events that followed

[1] *Return from the U.S.S.R.* first appeared in 1936, followed a year later by *Afterthoughts on the U.S.S.R.*

proved only too convincingly the accuracy of my account and even the correctness of my forecasts. But as for the trip itself, none that I ever took left me with more exhilarating memories. There is probably no country to which I have more ardently longed to go back. It must of course be admitted that I traveled throughout Russia as if carried, wafted along, on a wave of popular enthusiasm that was most exciting. Pierre Herbart used to take pleasure in claiming (chiefly to twit our guide Bola) that our car, or at least the one that preceded us, carried along with us the banners in my honor under which we passed as we entered each new village. But the enthusiasm, the exuberant cordiality of the reception, wherever I went . . . I may truly say that I tasted what is called fame, and that its taste is not always good. For if the show suddenly stopped as I entered the theater in Leningrad or Moscow to let the orchestra burst into the "*Marseillaise*" the moment I was seen, or when I approached cultural recreation-centers, how much more I was touched by the almost clandestine pleasures I enjoyed by the way when, thanks to the connivance of my traveling-companions, I managed to escape the untiring surveillance of those we called our "guardian angels."

Besides, that game of hide-and-seek did not lack charm in itself, although it was somewhat risky. People have even gone so far as to say that I was considerably thwarted, considerably bothered by the new laws against homosexuality that were rigorously observed, it seems, by the new regime. All I can say is that I was hardly aware of them, and that in no other country did I ever find such indulgence and connivance in that regard. To be sure, this was not to the devil's disadvantage. Besides, without being fully aware of it, I enjoyed a special immunity. . . . But I could not insist on this point without giving far too indiscreet details. Decidedly, I was right not to note anything down.

Outside my two little books on the U.S.S.R., I believe I have already spoken of this, and perhaps more than once. I have a vague impression of having done so. Yes, an impression that in what I am now writing I often happen to repeat myself. This is what is irreverently called indulging in "anecdotage." I run that risk by accepting without close scrutiny anything that now comes to me, whether new reflections or recollections. But this is the inevitable hazard of the undertaking I proposed when I began writing in this notebook. Yet if I now try to sort out the spontaneous run of the mill, all is lost. The free-and-easy, random carelessness is gone. Alas, it is better to accept the repetitions, however frequent they may be. Another thing bothers me that comes from the lack of chronological order in my mind: certain recollections overlap, telescope, fuse together, so that there are overprintings. They are particularly powerful in dreams. If I live but a little while longer, the terrors and horrors of the two World Wars will eventually mingle in many regards. Just as, but only in dreams, my wife's face often subtly and almost mystically takes the place of my mother's without really surprising me. The outlines of the faces are not sharp enough to keep me from shifting from one to the other; my emotion is keen enough, but its cause is ill-defined. Indeed, the role played by each in my dreams is about the same: an inhibitory role. And this explains or motivates the substitution.

The question of dreams could easily carry me too far afield, and I don't want to give it too much space. Yet I should have much to say on this subject. I have always been subject to insomnia, at least since adolescence, as many intellectuals are. It's a matter of disposition; unfortunately, my daughter inherited that tendency. I can recall in detail the very few times when I have gone through the night at a single stretch, so to speak, and in the morning was surprised and astounded at the length of time spent totally unconscious. Once, for instance, at Douarnenez, I believe, after having crossed the Menez Home on foot. I had most exceptionally gone to sleep the moment my head hit the pillow, and eight hours later . . . "Why, it's daylight!" I felt as if I had been robbed to some extent, for the time spent in dreaming is not altogether wasted. But how tiring it often is, especially if one is conscious of it! Often the nights when I am most exhausted, when I tell myself that I am going to sleep at once, when I have the most urgent need to restore myself, sleep eludes me most effectively; and, after a sleepless night, I am amazed to feel still capable of going on living and working. It often happens that I stretch out on my bed fully dressed and cheat a little; I pretend to read and, despite the light, the book often slips from my hands; I drop off for an hour or two with the feeling that I have made up for that much at least. I do use sleeping-pills, but as little as possible for fear of becoming inured to them. . . . The last few months I have got into the habit of getting up after midnight, out of impatience, and of trying to get back to work, or at least to reading, until three or four in the morning. Then I occasionally fall into a heavy sleep, but well before seven o'clock sounds of housework waken me. On the other hand, for years now I have indulged in a siesta after lunch, from one to three. I think that is what allows me to "hold up" despite my sleepless nights. As a result I come to understand very well the regime of such as Balzac and Proust.[2] Dr. Boissier, who treated me at Lamalou when I was still a child,[3] did me the greatest service by saying in a solemn way: "You say that you can't sleep more than three or four hours a night. Well, then, try to convince yourself that you probably don't need any more." Cheered by those words and less worried, I slept better.

Generally, in the afternoon I fall into a deep sleep. I really sleep then. But at night I often spend a long time in a state of torpor midway between sleep and waking. And, for some time now, this is what happens. Dead tired, I stretch out on my

---

[2] Balzac and Proust were both known for doing most of their writing at night.

[3] At the age of twelve and a half, André Gide first went to Lamalou-le-Haut, where Dr. Boissier treated his nervous disorders with mineral baths.

bed without undressing. I try to continue some reading or other in the hope that it will lead naturally to sleep. My book is under the bright light, and I am not aware that my eyes close. The surprising thing is that I go on reading—not the book itself, but a garland of printed words that I invent as I go along, reading and hearing them simultaneously. That lasts for several minutes, sometimes for a quarter of an hour. Then the book falls from my hands. Suddenly I come to and note that the invented text has no relation to what is contained in the book, to which I again give my attention. Then the gradual substitution is renewed. But the surprising thing is that what I invent nevertheless makes sense. I have even gone so far as to invent a whole series of pages in this way. Sometimes it is a speech I am giving. At others, it is a musical score I am reading and playing (and with what amazing virtuosity!). At one and the same time I follow the text and hear it. At other times it is a comic text whose humor takes me so by surprise that my own laughter wakens me. And I recall having already spoken of this fact, which remains incomprehensible to me: that one can one-self supply all the elements of surprise and still be taken by surprise. . . .[4] All the same, it's all very tiring; and I cannot read without a certain jealousy these lines by Descartes in a letter to Guez de Balzac (15 April 1631): "Here I sleep ten hours every night without being awakened by anything." After that I can still admire the *Discours de la Méthode* just as much, but I feel justified in thinking: obviously!

The blank page lies in front of me. My intention is to write anything whatever on it. But at once I become aware that I am not free. Everything checks and holds me back. First, the many daily cares. Then, above all, yesterday's impetus. I am led on a string, and it's all up with chance. And I try to convince myself that something altogether unmotivated is (would be) something utterly insignificant. In the past I had utilized what I used to call *imaginary interviews*.[5] Why did I not take advantage of them to relate this, which probably

[4] He discusses surprise in dreams, with two highly amusing examples, in his *Journals* under date of 21 November 1928.

[5] In the early years of this century, Gide occasionally expressed his ideas in the form of imaginary interviews (chiefly in *L'Ermitage* in 1905), a form to which he returned during the German occupation of France (in the literary supplement of *Le Figaro* in 1941 and 1942).

flattered my ego more than any compliment ever addressed to me? During a side trip that we were accustomed to take from Pontigny to Vézelay under the leadership of Paul Desjardins,[6] we had paused at Avallon and were looking into an antique shop which, among various objects, exhibited a few so-called "secondhand" books. To our surprise, one of them was the first edition of my *Porte étroite* in the blue-paper cover modeled on the second edition of Gérard de Nerval's *Faust*.[7] Already by that time that first edition had become rare, and Desjardins had gone into the shop with us, planning to give the little book to one of the students with us. He already had the book in his hands (I was beside him) when a very young girl, who suddenly seemed to me charming, rushed

---

[6] Before the First World War, Paul Desjardins (1859–1940) organized annual summer meetings of literary men from all over Europe at the abandoned Abbey of Pontigny in Burgundy. Each *décade,* or ten-day period, during the vacation months was devoted to a different topic; and Gide was one of the most regular attendants from the earliest years until the late thirties.

[7] With his novel *L'Immoraliste* in 1902, Gide adopted for most of his first editions an attractive small format with dark-blue cover ornamented with black type and delicate border. He had found the model in the second edition of Nerval's translation of *Faust,* a typically handsome book of the Romantic period, and always had a special affection for this particular presentation of his works, whether published by the Mercure de France or the *N.R.F.*

up blushing to the shopkeeper and, in a trembling but very distinct voice, whispered: "Oh! please, Papa . . . don't sell that one."

Immediately afterward I told myself that I should have got ahead of Desjardins, bought the book, and given it, with a suitable autograph, to that exquisite girl who seemed to have stepped out of a Balzac novel. But I am utterly lacking in presence of mind. Besides, identifying myself would have embarrassed the child, her father, the student, Desjardins, and me too. The shopkeeper took back the book: "Excuse me, this book got into that lot by mistake. . . ." We left empty-handed, but I with my heart bursting. Let me repeat that I don't think any praise ever touched me so much.

I see her now with pigtails. I hope I didn't invent this touch. . . . Oh, it's not at all that I'm trying to dress up an incident, but it becomes spontaneously simplified in my mind to the point of leaving only the essential in my memory. I imagine that certain novelists must be bothered by the minuteness with which they recall certain details, so that the indispensable is, as it were, smothered. The *erosion of outlines* that Nietzsche says is characteristic of classical writers takes place in me

112

naturally. I repeat this to myself to console myself for my shortcomings and, through optimism,
to turn to my credit what might otherwise distress
me. For instance, in my *Porte étroite* I spoke of
the little cross that Alissa wore—a cross of ame-
thysts, I had called it. I learned later on that it was
a cross of emeralds. I am not sure of having made
the change in the latest editions. I call upon my
readers to do so. Obviously, there is nothing important about this, on condition that it is not intentional.[8]

Huge chunks of the past leave the field of my
consciousness in this way, as if I had never really
lived them. If they have left any trace, I am unaware of it. Fortunately I have some friends whose
memory is better than mine. But some fragments
remain that I cannot manage to attach to one
another; and yet, if I may express it this way, they
all carry the same trade-mark, though it is almost

---

[8] Some of Gide's friends did think the change was intentional: Jean Schlumberger in his *Madeleine et André Gide* at-
tributes it to a desire not to identify Alissa with Madeleine.
The fact is that, although Gide refers to it as an "emerald cross"
in a journal entry of August 1922 reserved for posthumous
publication in *Et nunc manet* (*Madeleine*), he apparently
never made the change in any edition of *Strait Is the Gate*.
Even the most recent one, of February 1958, still has "ame-
thyst cross."

effaced. On the other hand, others are still almost dazzlingly vivid: I recall not only what was said and done, but even the very quality of the air. . . . Like that day when the auto left Marc Allégret and me on the edge of that stretch of water overgrown with unknown forms of vegetation, where the double escort of our porters was waiting for us. We eventually touched land and, along a path so narrow that two could not walk abreast, launched out under the heavy foliage of the mysterious forest we had to cross before reaching our first stopping-place.[9] It is one of the moments of my life I should most like to relive. We still thought innocently that everything would become stranger and stranger, and that the further we advanced into the woods, the more that enchanted forest would wrap us in its charms. But subsequently we found nothing more disconcerting. . . . But why talk of that moment rather than of so many others! At such moments it seems that time has come to a stop. Or at least one would like it to come to a stop. But the most insignificant

---

[9] Gide's detailed impressions of the Congo—in which he traveled for a full year in 1925–6 with young Marc Allégret, the son of his onetime tutor—can be found in his *Travels in the Congo.*

hours last neither more nor less than the others, however hard it may be to convince oneself of this. And, furthermore, it is known today that the brain is impressed by them just as by the others that leave a conscious trace; and there are known to be chemical means of temporarily reviving images that were supposed to be forgotten. Oh, how precious the faculty of forgetting seems to me! And that almost involuntary, at least instinctive, choice, so necessary to the outline of the human face with which we must make our journey through life and then quit life with the least possible baggage. What good is so much clutter to me?

I have known certain persons (they are numerous) in whom everything is a contribution from the outside; at least everything seems so, for it is unthinkable that there is not some tiny substratum in them around which the acquired can agglutinate. But there is nothing unintentional in them; they are built up of bits and pieces. They say: I detest this; I adore that; and you feel that it isn't true. They are simply basted together, and you have merely to pull on the thread for it to break and the patch to fall. Their feelings are motivated, and the more they protest of their friendship, the less you should believe in it. I like those who don't really know why they like what they like (and in such cases the liking is genuine).

The first type provides rather good heroes for bad novels. For it is never hard for a novelist to fashion a character who is utterly consistent with himself. Reality offers more frequent inconsistencies or, at very least, less apparent consistencies. It is in this regard that Balzac interests me less than Dostoevsky. This by way of digression, without the slightest implication that I consider Balzac a poor novelist. At most I should say that he constructs his characters too carefully and too rarely lets them take him by surprise.

A good pen plays a large part in the pleasure I take in writing. A year ago last spring I got myself a dictaphone. I haven't yet found out how to use it. And yet everything I am setting down in these notebooks should spring straightaway from my heart and brain without any polishing. Faced with that recording device, I can produce nothing but vacuous remarks I should be ashamed of, and in advance I judge them harshly. What I should like to entrust to the dictaphone would be dialogues. I am still waiting for the opportunity. There are amazing ones. But the time to set up the device, to place oneself and the willing interlocutor . . .

We should particularly like to have, not so much monologues of great men, even if they were Racine and Pascal, as their conversations, discussions between Montaigne and La Boétie, rambling conversations among Racine, La Fontaine, and Boileau, or even with Father Bouhours,[1] like the interview, so wonderfully noted down, of Bernardin de Saint-Pierre on a visit to Jean-Jacques.[2] That is what would really inform us. But everything sinks into the past, even what we are taking care to note down today.

I cannot think without terror of the piling up of "new publications" in the Bibliothèque Nationale.[3] The day will come, and perhaps it is not far off,

[1] The three great writers of the classical age, Jean Racine (1639–99), Jean de La Fontaine (1621–95), and Nicholas Boileau-Despréaux (1636–1711), were close friends. The Jesuit priest Father Bouhours (1628–1702) was a literary critic and arbiter of style whose advice Racine often took. Indeed, Gide did write an imaginary dialogue between Racine and Father Bouhours which appears in his *Journals* for 1918.

[2] The delightful account of a visit to Rousseau in June 1772, in which the man, his apartment, and his remarks are described with scrupulous accuracy, appears under the title of *"Essai sur J.-J. Rousseau"* in the posthumous works of the novelist and naturalist Bernardin de Saint-Pierre (1737–1814).

[3] According to law, a copy of every book published in France must be deposited in the National Library in Paris.

when some frightful cataclysm will reduce all that
to ashes. And if anything survives, it will not be
necessarily the best. On the basis of what flotsam
will our civilization, our culture, be judged later
on? On the basis of Rodin or on the basis of
Dufayel? [4] I made the serious mistake, when I was
young and in a position to buy, of supposing that
the books which today I deplore not having in my
library would always be available and that I should
only have to ask a bookseller for them. But just go
out now and try to get the collection, so valuable
today, of plays republished by the Mermaid! [5]
And the little set of Dickens, of Meredith, of Hardy
—to speak only of the English. At last an excellent
new edition of Renan makes a little space on the
overloaded shelves. Likewise for the Pléiade collection, which, moreover, became rather rare, some
of them at least, almost at once. [6] But I maintain

[4] Gide is contrasting here the sculpture of Auguste Rodin
(1840–1917) with the Grand Rapids type of furniture sold by
the Dufayel department store on the installment plan.

[5] The Mermaid Series published in London "The Best Plays
of the Old Dramatists"—such as Congreve, Dryden, Ford,
Ben Jonson, and Marlowe.

[6] Because of the India paper on which it is printed, the de-
finitive edition of Renan's *Œuvres complètes,* edited by Hen-
riette Psichari, will come to but ten volumes when finished.
The first three or four volumes had appeared by the time of
Gide's writing this. The Pléiade collection of classics from the

118

that a young student of today has trouble really educating himself. A country that was seriously concerned with its traditions and its culture, as ours ought to be (until the exterminating cataclysm comes), ought to do more to help him. If, in order to read a classic, he must go without a meal, it is obvious that he will think about it twice. And slowly but surely the barbarous state wins out. At the time of my childhood we didn't know how happy we were. O lost paradises! And to think that there are fewer and fewer who regret them. Only when deprived of some advantage does one begin to assess its value. But I am speaking here of just those values which cannot be assessed. No, decidedly I am not gay every day. . . .

If I show this, I do so to identify myself more closely with the reader, for I feel no need to flaunt my lamentation. I think that one of the chief reasons for my own sorrow (to say nothing of what is due to external events) is the thoughtless ease with which we let ourselves be distracted; we simply let

Bible and Homer through Gide, Valéry, and Malraux was founded by Jacques Schiffrin and later taken over by the Gallimard publishing-house at the instigation of Gide and Schlumberger. Printed on thin paper and leather-bound, the volumes are compact and authoritatively edited.

go. Our embrace cannot be so broad as not to let drop many assets which belong (which belonged at least) to our patrimony; but this involves no choice. Suddenly a generation casts off certain, often excellent, masters. What takes place? Nothing so ridiculous as those so-called laws which some theorists have tried to establish—laws according to which every writer, almost immediately after his death, would have to plunge into a momentary neglect. In their calculations the question of a work's value almost never enters. Those so-called laws were invented out of charity, out of politeness, out of vanity also—rather than to confess that we have to admit today, despite all our hastily bestowed praise, that Mr. X's work is valueless, that we were wrong about its value. Now, by the way, I consider that one of the most remarkable virtues of the old *N.R.F* was that it almost never made a mistake about the real value of the writers it had to discuss.[7] I shall never give up this opinion: a healthy criticism—creative, quickening, and pro-

---

[7] The *Nouvelle Revue Française* was from the first proud of its reviews and critical notes, which established the criteria for French literature of several generations. See *From the N.R.F.*, edited by Justin O'Brien.

tecting—necessarily, during the most prosperous periods, accompanies the loftiest products of the mind. And those who claim to depreciate criticism in favor of something wild and intractable are simpletons. Nonetheless, it is essential never to leave alone (or to rely upon) the so-called precepts it imposes upon us. (I should prefer: never to let oneself be taken in by them.) [8]

It does not seem to me that criticism has ever been better exercised in any country than in France. I ought to substitute for my "better" the word "more" so as to explain by a natural progression a certain drying up of the poetic faculty (which I admire England for not having known: it does not seem to me open to question that Pope was a more important poet than Boileau).

The disadvantage to such ratiocinations is that they are necessarily infinite. And one of the major conveniences of the *Journals* was that the very form authorized closing the sluice gate before the flow ran dry. There is no occasion to return to that form now, for I am well aware that if I begin again

---

[8] There is a play here on the expressions *laisser en repos* ("leave alone"), *se reposer sur* ("rely upon"), and *s'en laisser imposer* ("be impressed by").

to set down dates opposite what I am aiming to write in a continuous way, I shall fall back at once into the same pitfalls.

But inasmuch as this is not a *Journal*, I want to take advantage of the license granted by this piece of writing to speak again (I enjoy doing so) of the wonderful child who was a part of our escort when we crossed the Cameroons. I have already said a few words about him in the account of my *Travels in the Congo*, but not enough, and cannot cease regretting Marc Allégret's negligence when he could so easily have taken his photograph. It would have kept my imagination from straying somewhat, as it now does for want of reference points. . . . In addition to the obligatory escort of our porters, Sultan Reï Bouba, without warning us, had added to them two young pages as mere extras. The fact was unprecedented, but probably justified the great reputation for kindness that earlier travelers' accounts had passed on to us. Nevertheless, that kindness had a quite different basis. Sultan Reï Bouba's benevolence, constantly guided by a superior intelligence, had managed to make of his Sultanate a sort of favored state, an enclave in the midst of a region converted to Islam but still rather primitive. That the

122

considerable moral and social arrangements instituted by the Sultan were always approved by our French authorities, I am in no position to assert (besides, what I saw goes back to 1925, and many things may have changed since). But I can state that felicity and exhilaration could be read on the faces of the citizens of that little country when we went through it. We regretted not being able to tarry there. Having taken leave of the Sultan in the evening, we set out for N'Gaoundéré rather early the next day, and were keenly surprised to notice soon among our porters two youths whose sole function seemed to be to escort us. Let me add at once that they were as handsome as possible, real luxury creatures. Certainly the Sultan had chosen them. Each of them walked along at a little distance, as if belonging to our troop and yet not mingling with it, as if not deigning to mingle with it. Moreover, hardly conversing with each other. Less to burden him than to give him a semblance of justification, we had decided to entrust to the younger one Dindiki's empty cage.[9] In addi-

---

[9] *Le Retour du Tchad* (which forms part of *Travels in the Congo*) describes Mala more briefly but similarly. Dindiki was a small lemur that Gide tamed in the Congo and hoped to bring back to the zoo, but unfortunately the creature died before this stage of the journey.

tion to that, he bore, as his elder did, an almost childish bow slung over his shoulder and, on his back like Cupid, a quiver with several arrows. Both of them wearing a sort of toque on their heads. A leather belt kept the younger one's smock from falling below mid-thigh length. Both of them looked as if they had stepped down from the fresco in the Campo Santo of Pisa, ready to take part in Benozzo Gozzoli's grape harvest. Their gait, especially that of the younger one, had something of the dancer's spring; he was Nijinsky, for the muscle's joy became apparent and we, spectators, took part in it. Surely it was not exclusively for our eyes' pleasure that the Sultan had lent us his two pages. This is what I did not cease repeating to myself for three days. Finally I made up my mind to talk freely to my faithful Adoum. But, before going farther, it is well to insert a parenthesis.

It scarcely seems possible to me that Reï Bouba was informed of my tastes. Had they been different, as Marc's were, would the Sultan have been inclined to take out of his private harem two women to accompany us on our long marches? Allow me to doubt it. And to run the risk of complications of all sorts! These two adolescents didn't commit the Sultan or us to anything. We were free to pay no attention to them, as my companion did. But inasmuch as I saw this as a most gracious attention on the part of the Sultan, it didn't seem to me right to appear to scorn it. The pages themselves appeared to be hurt by our lack of attention, by not being noticed more, for their good spirits decreased from day to day. What? Was this all we thought of them? So that the fourth morning, giving up my resistance and swallowing my shame, I asked Adoum how to go about it, for, after all, I was never alone, and the least thing I did was seen by the whole troop of porters. . . . Adoum found my embarrassment hard to understand. He asserted that every one of the porters would consider it quite natural that some evening I should ask one of the two pages to "come and wield the punkah" under my mosquito net. Let it be quickly added that it is impossible to see through the fabric of a mosquito net. It should also be added that the heat was stifling, so that the desire to have one's sleep fanned by a punkah could seem almost natural. And finally let it be added that what seemed most natural was what the expression "come and wield the punkah" signified in reality, so that no one in our group was struck by it. And in order to destroy completely any attempt at dissimulation, Mala (that was the boy's name) began by ridding himself in a hot tub of the sweat and dust of a long march, as I had just done myself. Sweet little Mala! On my deathbed I should like to see again your elfin laugh and your joy.

Little do I care if these words shock some, who will consider them impious. I have promised myself to override that. But I should like to be more sure than I am that, if I should happen to reread them, I shall not be embarrassed by them myself. Is it really around the least spiritual in me that my final thoughts will collect? When it might still be time, perhaps, to offer them to the God awaiting me, as you say, in whom I refuse to believe? In a moment the game will be up, without possible retouching. All will be over, and for all eternity! Why! all *has* been over for some time now, I am tempted to reply, and to disown in advance any recantation brought about by the confusion of the death agony. But I should like to protest also against any excessive limitation one might be tempted to see in this profession of materialism. I do not intend thereby to confine myself to mere carnal pleasure; it invites me to melt into and merge with surrounding nature. This is why my most perfect memories of sensual delight are those enveloped in a landscape which absorbs it and in which I seem to be swallowed up. In the one I have just evoked of those transports with Mala, it is not only the beautiful swooning body of the child I see again, but the whole mysterious and fearful surrounding of the equatorial forest.

During a memorable nocturnal conversation (there were not so many that I cannot recall each one) Proust explained to me his concern to gather together, by means of the orgasm, the most incongruous sensations and emotions. The pursuit of the rats, among others, could be justified in this way;[1] in any case, Proust urged me to see it thus. I saw it rather as the admission of a sort of physiological deficiency. To achieve satisfaction, how many extra ingredients he had to have! But which, indirectly, serve to provide his books with their amazingly profuse complexity.

People insist that I should be Claudel's enemy. That he owes it to himself to be mine is not quite the same thing. I am not at all averse to his taking

---

[1] André Germain in *Les Clés de Proust* tells how Proust used to have a number of rats brought into his room together with a group of young men to chase the rats and beat them until they bled. If not from Germain, Gide might have heard this tale from his friend Bernard Faÿ, who told it to Germain.

his stand against me. What an odd state of mind
he has! On the side opposite the Church he can
see nothing but insignificant twaddle. Yet not so
stupid but that he realizes . . . Realizes what?
That the sole enemy of what he considers the
Truth is not intellectual conceit. My admiration
for certain bursts of his genius is just the same as
it was in my youth, and his most insulting denials
cannot change it in any way.[2] He alone ought to
be embarrassed by them. And even more because
unbelievers are not the only ones to be annoyed
by the triumphant Catholicism he incarnates.
Claudel aims to win out on every score. Is it surprising that a Bernanos, profoundly Christian and
open to suffering, should become indignant and
wonder if it is possible to reach Paradise in a Pull-
man car? Nothing is more foreign to me than Claudel's spirit of domination. His lyricism finds nour-
ishment in his belief; yet when he does without
his belief, he is at his greatest, in my opinion, with

---

[2] Probably the most insulting remarks Claudel made publicly
about Gide appeared in an interview Dominique Arban had
with Claudel in March 1947. Published first in the newspaper
Combat, it was reproduced at the end of the correspondence
between Claudel and Gide. After refusing to recognize any
talent in Gide, Claudel added: "From the artistic point of view,
from the intellectual point of view, Gide doesn't count."

all due deference to him; and less great when he looks for compromises. Some of his interpretations of the Bible are ridiculous, ludicrous, and so likely to repel people that one feels grateful to him for urging them upon us like warning guard-rails: let us not be led along that path, even through instinctive attraction.

If some success comes to *Les Caves du Vatican* in the near future, Claudel will be furious; not so much against the book or the play as against the public, as he was at the time of the Nobel Prize. As it is proved by "the Scriptures" that I have no talent and could not have any, any attention that is granted me can only be the result of intrigue. Faith has no concern with whatever violence it is necessarily called upon to do to truth (I should say to others' truths, for the Church possesses the only Truth). "A Protestant clique," Claudel said of the Nobel jury. Great analogy with the Communist cult: you can enter the house only after leaving outside your gumption, common sense, and critical spirit—all freedom of thought.

I interrupt myself to catch my breath. To tell the truth, I am interrupted by the production of the *Caves du Vatican* at the Comédie-Française. Everything is going along wonderfully, despite my excessive fatigue. A complete dedication on everyone's part rewards my least efforts. I feel strengthened, encouraged, often guided by M. Touchard, the Administrator, beside whom I enjoy sitting during some of the last rehearsals and who never gives me any advice that does not suit my intentions, so that it is to my advantage to follow him. As for Jean Meyer, I could not have wished for a more supple, more intelligent director and interpreter; almost excessively deferential; at one and the same time getting inside his part and dominating it sufficiently to see the whole play in perspective. . . . I could go on praising him endlessly. I could easily say the same for each of the actors. And this leads me to think that the feeling that bursts most spontaneously from my heart is gratitude. It rather overwhelms me, and often I have trouble not showing it in exaggerated demonstrations. It could almost seem an effect of senility. But it is not a matter of age: I know that my daughter, Catherine, has to make the same effort, not so much to choke back her tears as to repress the sob that seizes her when confronted with anything whatever that rises above vulgar flabbiness, anything whatever revealing human nobility, majesty, dignity. I recall, going far back into the past (it was in . . . , at La Brévine, where I was writing *Paludes* and my friend Eugène Rouart had come to spend a few days with me).[3] One morning he told me he had overheard a sentence I expressed in my sleep, with deep emotional intensity, in a very loud voice so that I had wakened him though he was sleeping in the next room: "Yes! Yes! Yes! Mankind is wonderful." We could well laugh about it the next day, but those unconscious words revealed my secret and basic thought. "Nobility, dignity, majesty". . . I am afraid and almost ashamed to use these expressions, so shamelessly have they been misused. Wrenched as they are today, they seem almost obscene words—like all noble words, moreover, such as the word "virtue" to begin with. But it is not only the words that have become debased, it is also what they mean: the meaning of these words has changed, and their devaluation merely makes flagrant the general collapse of all that seemed to us sacred, of all that encouraged us to live, of all that saved us

---

[3] Gide wrote *Paludes* (*Marshlands*) during the winter of 1894–5 at La Brévine, a Swiss village high in the Jura Mountains. Years later he described that snowbound, inhospitable village as the setting for his *Pastoral Symphony*.

from despair. The Christian gets along all right, as we know; and the Moslem, and all those who are willing to close their eyes and believe in some superhuman power, in some god concerned about each one of us. Through mere human reason some cannot accept that too easy consolation. Therefore they must seek and find their resource in themselves alone. And even if a little pride enters into this, is it not legitimate? And the austere and noble feeling of duty properly fulfilled, of the restoration in oneself of a man's potentialities, of what allows the tortured man to look at his torturer and think: you are the victim.

Oh, to be sure, I am well aware that it is easy for me to talk of all this, sitting calmly far from the fight; but does thought deserve to be propagated when distorted and under duress? What I am writing freely now I want to see set up in the future against what I may be forced to say. For I have no idea whether or not my weak flesh is the stuff of which martyrs are made. And, besides, they have such clever means, today, of undermining the will itself and of turning the hero into a docile and debased instrument!

And since I have interrupted myself, I should

like to explain myself somewhat. For, after all, I should not like anyone to be misled: I continue to note down in this book everything that goes through my head. It so happens that almost no trace appears here of the dreadful events upsetting everything round about and threatening to change the face of the world. Is this tantamount to saying that they leave me indifferent? It is easy for Valéry, in his closed system, to write: "Events do not interest me"; and I understand very well what he means by that. It is not quite the same with me. I take an interest—I even occasionally claim to take a part—in "what happens"; but, to tell the truth, I must confess that I do not really succeed in believing in it. I don't know how to explain this, though for a very perspicacious reader it must, I think, already emerge from my writings (besides, I have at times noted it explicitly): I don't hit it off, I have never been able to hit it off completely with reality.[4] Properly speaking, it is not even a

---

[4] In 1924 Gide noted in his *Journals:* "I can be extremely sensitive to the outer world, but I never succeed completely in believing in it. What I am saying has nothing theoretical about it. . . . I can imagine that a very learned doctor would be able to discover that some 'internally secreting gland,' some 'adrenal capsule' is atrophied in me."

result of dissociation that someone, in me, is always an observer of the one who acts. No, it is the very one who acts, or who suffers, who doesn't take himself seriously. I even believe that at the moment of death I shall say to myself: "Look! He's dying." Hence, suffering round about can come closer and closer and lay siege to my door; I am as moved by it as anyone can be (and sometimes even, sometimes, I think, more than if I were involved), and I tend to it and become wrought up about it, but it doesn't take its place among real things. I think this failing (for obviously it is one) must be linked to what I said above: a lack of the feeling of *time*. Whatever happens to me, or to someone else, I immediately put it in the past. Enough to distort seriously judgment about events destined to become historical. I bury people and things, and myself, with disconcerting ease; the only thing I keep (oh! unintentionally) is their meaning. And, judging from the way the world is going, I keep repeating to myself that these ratiocinations may well, before long, be swept away with all the rest. But I nonetheless write them, just like little Hauviette in Péguy's *Jeanne d'Arc*, who declares that if the last day were imminent, if "the angel were beginning to blow his trumpet" she would neither more nor less go on playing *boquillons* [5] as if nothing were happening.

We are both witnesses and actors today of a vast tragic farce, and no one knows what will come of it. We have been surfeited with horror, and the farce is not near its end yet. Thousands of persons have been confronted with the question: is it my duty to say yes or no? The question still calls for an answer, but with the dreadful certainty that their acceptance or rejection will hardly matter at all. But what does matter is each of them taken individually. It is important for each of them to be able to die satisfied with himself and without having forsworn himself. If the problem should arise likewise for me, all of a sudden, I should not know how to solve it . . . and should go back to playing *boquillons* until I began to understand better.

A few words more, however. At Cuverville the young wife of our gardener Marius died suddenly. He was still very young himself, and I was more attached to him than to any other servant, especially as at that time I paid great attention to the garden, so that I helped him daily in his work. He

---

[5] From the old Picard form *bosc* for modern *bois, boquillons* is a picturesque term for "woodsmen" and doubtless the name for a children's game in the Middle Ages.

was deeply moved by his loss, to which I was very sensitive too, for a more prepossessing young wife or a more devoted couple could not be imagined. A few of us went to the little farmhouse close by, where the dead woman lay surrounded by flowers and sprigs of holly. Marius stood motionless at the head of the bed, rooted in a pose of great dignity. I shook his hand without saying a word, too deeply moved to be able to speak. I don't know how to explain that my wife was not there; but probably she had come before us. Her sister Jeanne Drouin began to talk to Marius, and found in her heart numerous wonderful remarks, or which at least seemed so to me, said in exactly the right tone of voice, full of pity, consolation, and hope: the young wife was waiting for him in heaven, where, even now, she had taken her place among the angels; she was thinking of the husband she had left behind, whom she was constantly watching over, loving, and protecting, while singing beautiful hymns. . . . And I was full of wonder that religion could provide such a sincere outpouring of feeling, whereas all my friendship for Marius furnished me nothing to say. As for knowing what Marius thought of it . . . ?!

I admire all forms of holiness (even though some

nauseate me), but Claudel did well to educate me by the amazing letter he wrote me about my *Porte étroite* pointing out the Protestant heresy in the fact of loving good independently of the promised reward.[6] He subsequently made clear in a conversation that the Catholic must humbly love and practice virtue *because* . . . and that my Huguenot pride rebelled against the bargain, the agreement with God, the tit for tat. In the beginning I was surprised, almost angry, upon seeing that sort of bookkeeping. Subsequently it greatly helped to open my eyes and show me that the whole system of indulgences and of "assuring one's salvation" depends on it. It was better to break off, and that is what I did.

There are two distinct worlds. I can well imagine Noah in his Ark writing the *Ethics* or the *Discourse on Method* just as if contrary tides were not flooding the universe. People sometimes express amazement at the little echo that Napoleon's conquests

---

[6] In a letter of 10 May 1909 from China, after having read *Strait Is the Gate,* Claudel spoke of "that old Quietist blasphemy, nauseatingly repeated throughout the last century, according to which piety needs no reward, since the noblest love is the most disinterested." "God's gifts are not distinct from his essence," he added. "To refuse one is to reject the other. Loving without having any interest in doing so would be a sorry love."

awoke in French letters. Today things are less compartmented, but I doubt if there is any reason to rejoice at this. Each of us is more or less involved in the general anguish, and it may seem monstrously selfish to try to avoid it. The writings of the present (and I am speaking even of the best) suffer a sort of contamination which I, for one, consider degrading. The plague was ravaging Florence and every day brought fresh griefs while Boccaccio was writing his *Decameron*. I don't dream of taking refuge in a delightful villa at Fiesole so as to be able to look down with impunity on the calamity. No indeed; if events force me, I am ready to face them. I shall try not to dishonor myself, not to tremble too much when confronting the horror. But don't ask me to assume a false voice and introduce quavers into my writing through expedience. . . .

What more should I say? That everything I am writing here strikes me as valueless, for I am speaking only of general calamities whereas there are nothing but individual cases, despite the claims of Communism. I think that is true especially for France and England, and that Germany, just like Russia, can standardize itself much more easily and painlessly than we ever could. I also believe that a collective ideology is more easily applicable anywhere else than with us. But events convince us that, even if ideological, the great Russian rallying has taken place, or will still take place, not around the idea of theoretical socialism, but rather thanks to the revived concept of nation. Yes, of nation, with everything involved that was supposed to be swept away, including the concept of religion; and Stalin made no mistake about it.

I am subject myself to that contamination which I was just mentioning . . . and, while I am about it, how can one continue to take seriously Pascal's assertion about the truth of any opinion whatever being proved by the gift of oneself? In a conflict people get killed on both sides without its *proving* anything at all. In that case, I prefer Galileo with his *"Eppur si muove."* Yet one would so much like to know and be convinced that one's own sacrifice (that of any private soldier whatever) at least serves some purpose. This is where a little mysticism would be welcome.

I should give my life so that God might be. Yes, that is all right. But: I give my life to prove that God is—is not right at all; this ceases to have any meaning whatever. But we are no longer on a theosophical plane today. Thousands of people are

ready to give their lives to bring about a better
state of things on earth: for more justice, for a better distribution of material wealth. I don't dare
add: for more liberty, because I don't really know
what is meant by that.

In any case, keeping quiet is not at all tantamount to being indifferent. Those who approach
me are well aware of this. The only question I have
a right (I was about to say: a duty) to ask myself
is: what good can I be? For this is where we stand:
amid such universal distress (if not universal, it
spares only the privileged, only the happy few to
which one is loath or ashamed to belong), how
can one reduce that distress somewhat? That is
the problem, and in face of it I know and feel that
I can do almost nothing. During the First World
War, I had wisely made up my mind to keep
silent and to devote all my time to helping refu-
gees; at least that kept me from thinking of anything else.[7] American gifts poured in to us; we were
simply the dispensing agency; but examining each
case of need kept us so busy that we had no leisure

[7] Declared unsuited for military service because of age and
health, Gide devoted himself heart and soul during the First
World War to alleviating suffering as assistant head of the
Foyer Franco-Belge.

at all. I do not think it would have been possible to be more zealously and conscientiously concerned with others than some of us were for months. Dare I speak cynically? With few exceptions, the cases of destitution we helped were not very interesting. I mean that nothing but their need fixed our attention and our interest on the lamentable derelicts who came to us. What a school of misanthropy! At times, but very rarely, a glimmer kept us from thinking: what's the use? Almost all of those to whom we gave the means of going on living seemed to us lamentable dregs of humanity. Let it be added at once that almost every one of them showed himself in his least favorable aspect, in the most unattractive light. Sometimes, during my visits to their lodgings, I happened to discover, next to our applicants, more authentic needs which, through modesty and common decency, were reluctant to show themselves; immediately we would direct all our attention to the latter. But even then, what were we in a position to know except by-products of the war, moraines worn away from their position on the edge of a glacier? At that time there was not yet the mixing up of whole nations, the concentration camps, the inhuman atrocities that the following war gave us.

During the initial months of the second war, exclusively concerned with providing political exiles the means of fleeing to America, I was immediately confronted with people who were often kept merely by their feeling of human dignity from giving in and keeping a comfortable situation in Germany, when the racial question did not enter in. (Even then, I had to take all the precautions provided by the secret police, for espionage was constantly to be feared.) No matter; I was dealing with a picked group; I was offering the gangplank that was in my power to people who deserved to be saved, for I had proof of this. Individual cases were involved. On the other hand, nothing was more disappointing (with a few rare exceptions) than that almost indistinct generosity, despite all the means of checking that our desire for equity and our need for discrimination invented. This question was constantly rising before me: what good to society is this flabby and amorphous creature in whom I cannot yet discern (I vainly probe) the tiniest spark of the sacred fire? . . . No matter. I had ingloriously taken on a task, as unspectacular as I could have wished it, which I was eager to fulfill punctually to the limits of the moral contract, and this is what I did without flinching, though to the point of nausea. But it was essential to me to prove to myself that I was someone who could be counted on.

Even more imperiously there arose before me, there still constantly arises, the question: what is, what can be, my best service? That my writings are there as an answer goes without saying; but I should like to make things a little clearer. For it is one thing to write and another to publish. Now, at least twice in my career what I had felt obliged to write was of such a nature as to leave some doubt about the timeliness of publishing without delay. It was on the occasion of my report on my trip in the U.S.S.R. and on the occasion of *Cory-don*.[8] In both cases I had written nothing but what was exact; and particularly for the U.S.S.R. events subsequently confirmed only too fully what I had

---

[8] Gide's Socratic dialogues in defense of homosexuality were first printed privately and anonymously in 1911 under the title of *C.R.D.N.*, then in less fragmentary form but under the same conditions in 1920. When the book finally appeared publicly in 1924 with the title *Corydon* and the author's name, Gide argued with his friends that the book *had* to be written, that he was uniquely qualified to write it, and that not to do so would amount to shirking his duty and countenancing false-hood.

put forth. "Yes," said certain friends who had remained Communists and even convinced Stalinists, "yes, we know only too well that you have said nothing that we are not obliged to recognize as true. But by divulging it you are playing into the hands of our worst enemies, who are also yours. . . . Wait until events make your publication timely." It didn't require much perspicacity to foresee, for sure, that such an appropriate occasion would never occur. I am omitting the other argument which some (and Claudel in particular) brought up in relation to *Corydon*, the shameful argument as I call it: "You will harm yourself." Why, of course, I had no doubt about this and was under no illusion either as to the unleashing of hatred that the publication of my *Retour de l'U.R.S.S.* would necessarily provoke. I was risking my tranquillity in both cases; but there is a certain form of moral comfort that it seemed to me I was paying too dearly for if I was doing so at the expense of veracity. I have explained myself at length on this subject, both for the *Retour de l'U.R.S.S.* and for *Corydon*. I have even related the visit from Maritain, who came to beg me to abandon the publication of a book which, according to him, might disturb, pervert, mislead souls insufficiently an-

chored by the Truths of the Church.[9] I was dealing
with a man of conviction whose sincerity should
have shaken me if, as far as I was concerned, I had
not been just as convinced that I had been right
to write it and was right to publish it. I think I can
say today that if I had given in, I should never
have forgiven myself. I have had many a proof
since then that that little book has saved many a
distracted person from despair.

So I come back to that question of the best service. It is certain that the man who wonders as he
takes up his pen: what service can be performed
by what I am about to write? is not a born writer,
and would do better to give up producing at once.
Verse or prose, one's work is born of a sort of im-
perative one cannot elude. It results (I am now
speaking only of the authentic writer) from an
artesian gushing-forth, almost unintentional, on
which reason, critical spirit, and art operate only
as regulators. But once the page is written, he may
wonder: what's the use? . . . And when I turn
to myself, I think that what above all urged me to
write is an urgent need of understanding. This is

---

[9] Gide's fascinating report of the conversation with the Catholic philosopher Jacques Maritain (1882–   ) on this occasion is in the *Journals* under date of 21 December 1923.

the need that now prompts the ratiocinations with which I am filling this notebook and makes me banish all bombast from them. I hope the young man who may read me will feel on an equal footing with me. I don't bring any doctrine; I resist giving advice; and in a discussion I beat a hasty retreat. But I know that today many seek their way gropingly and don't know in whom to trust. To them I say: believe those who are seeking the truth; doubt those who find it; doubt everything, but don't doubt of yourself. There is more light in Christ's words than in any other human word. This is not enough, it seems, to be a Christian: in addition, one must *believe*. Well, I do not believe. Having said this, I am your brother.

Some remarks I wrote at the beginning of the last war, or more exactly after the disaster and at the beginning of the occupation, were bitterly held against me. It would have been very simple for me not to publish them, and I was not unaware of the harm they might do me. But it struck me as unseemly to cheat by hiding my weaker moments. It is certain that for a rather long time I thought all was lost. I was alone then near Carcassonne, and nothing justified me in supposing that there was even a ghost of resistance. And an organization of resistance seemed to me even more fanciful. When I resumed contact with old friends at Nice and Cabris a little later, I began to realize that the game was not so completely lost as I had feared and that, in any case, some had made up their minds to play it out to the end with all its risks. In the beginning, for lack of information, I thought that some of the most spirited of our young people were blindly rushing toward obvious disaster. Their sacrifice might bring about a total hecatomb to no advantage whatsoever, and France would be just as impoverished, and even more bloodless, than it already was. For the first time, however, X's assurance, when he came to see me in Nice, his ardent and yet calm confidence, brought me a glimmer of hope.

A second visit, shortly afterward when I was at Cabris, strengthened that too timid hope, and my whole sky was lighted up by it. That second visit was from Boris Wilde, whom I had been lodging for months in a vacant room above mine on the sixth floor.[1] I don't know what happy coincidence had brought us together. As he was looking for a job, I had warmly recommended him to Paul Rivet,

[1] This was in Gide's Paris apartment at 1bis rue Vaneau.

who was then the head of the Musée de l'Homme at the Trocadéro. Rivet had the sense to recognize his exceptional value at once. Wilde stayed in the background, so discreet and reserved that I hardly knew him and could certainly not foresee the heroic part he was ready to play in the resistance. Yet, at the time of his visit at Cabris, the conversation he had with me that night seemed to me so important that I did not hesitate to put him in contact with Pierre Viénot, who was sleeping, or trying to sleep (he was suffering from a painful neuritis) in the room next to mine, in the house of his mother-in-law Mme Mayrisch, whose guest I was together with Jean Schlumberger.[2] Anxious not to be in their way, I withdrew after having introduced Viénot and Wilde to each other. Their conversation lasted until morning. Wilde had recently married. Just a few days after that meeting at Cabris, Wilde, surrounded, was shot at Saint-Etienne. I bow respectfully before his very noble figure.

[2] As a French statesman active in the Resistance, Pierre Viénot (1897–1944) became one of the first members of the Free French government in London, where he died. He was the son-in-law of Mme Mayrisch de Saint-Hubert, a woman of vast culture in several languages who made her castle of Colpach in Luxembourg, and later her estate on the Riviera, a meeting-place for artists and statesmen.

Those who knew him have a sort of veneration for that martyr.

During my very long absence, what had become of my apartment? [3] Occupied by reliable friends, it held in store certain surprises for me, at least my library. With what amused astonishment I discovered one day, some time after my return, behind the tight rows of La Curne de Sainte-Palaye, Forcellini, and many other volumes that one doesn't consult often (at least I don't), an extraordinary supply of papers, henceforth worthless, of seals, and of rubber stamps—enough to supply a whole army with false identities, and enough to justify shooting those who had taken on the rash mission of distributing them. Now that there was no reason to tremble about them, there was nothing to do but laugh about them. But I didn't know which to admire the more: the resolution and courage of the Resistants, or their patient force of dissimulation under trial, so that the secret did not get out and was kept as long as necessary to realize the most risky of undertakings. In this case the French revealed secret virtues of which I confess

---

[3] From the spring of 1940 until the spring of 1946 André Gide had been away from Paris, first on the South Coast and then in Algeria and Tunisia.

that I should not have thought them capable except in a quite exceptional way. Decidedly our honor was restored. The question henceforth facing us was quite different in nature: what could be and what was to be our role now in a new world? It was essential not only to resume and to strengthen our place, but also to reconstruct, and this had to be done on shifting sands. . . .

I was worried to the point of anguish by the spiritual confusion of the rising generation. The only example it had before its eyes was that of bankruptcies. Once it had slept off the initial intoxication of triumph, nothing seemed worth living for. Everywhere could be seen cheating, exploitation, corrupt practices; and words themselves had lost the authentic meaning around which one might have liked to rally. Eventually I realized that the only possible basis for agreement was negative in nature: there was what we were obliged to accept, at least temporarily, and what we positively refused to agree to: falsehood. O wiles, O subterfuges, O degrading compromises! Neither toward oneself nor toward others, whether it comes from the Left or the Right, whether Catholic or Communist, should one put up with falsehood.

What I am saying makes you smile? Well, then, this is because I am not saying it properly.

The farther human suffering is from us, the more abstract it becomes. I know many a charitable soul who ceases to be so at a distance. Whether that distance is in time or space. Of certain agonies those souls would dare to say, if they were really sincere: "But after all . . . it's too far away." Imagination falters when it is stretched too tight. We hear the S.O.S. sent out from the next house, but from beyond the first corner the brief call may not even reach us; and too much static gets in the way. There are also many people who are more sensitive to the imaginary than to the real, and who are more likely to sympathize with the sufferings of a fictional hero, if only they are well depicted, than with those beside them—which, to tell the truth, they don't really see.

Our potentialities for compassion are most often extraordinarily limited, sometimes used up almost at once. And it is such a mistake to think that a hundred misfortunes are a hundred times more moving than a single one! When not hundreds but thousands are concerned, one might as well give up at once. Consequently, when faced with huge

151

catastrophes, with too widespread disasters, our feeling changes: it is not pity but indignation that we feel, a revolt against the inacceptable: something must be changed. Then one begins to fight. There is no further possibility of withdrawing from the game. The gods have decidedly failed, and man himself must check humanity's collapse. The oddest thing is that that apparent collapse (could it be that it is not real?) coincides with an unexpected development of man's power, and that it would probably suffice if we were willing to apply that power properly. But some agreement would be necessary, and everything works for division. The threat grows and I tremblingly repeat to myself Shakespeare's line:

So foul a sky clears not without a storm.

I likewise repeat to myself the dialogue I read somewhere or other between an English district-leader in India and the doctor caring for the plague-ridden and fighting against the plague's terrifying progress:

"I have studied the question thoroughly and am convinced that very little expense would suffice to . . ."

The district-leader: "How many human lives do

you hope to save by taking these precautions?"

The doctor: "Naturally I can't be exact, but they would probably be counted in the tens of thousands."

The district-leader: "Allow me to believe that I know the question even better than you. In the region under my charge, those who are destined to die of hunger this summer will be counted by hundreds of thousands. Let the plague have its way, doctor. Thank you for your advice anyway. Meanwhile, read or reread Malthus."

I am dressing it up and simplifying, but don't really see what the doctor could have answered.

I had not made arrangements to live so old. From a certain age onward, it seemed to me that I was getting outside my role. My optimism became strained, or else it beat a retreat. I had to admit that the look of the world hardly justified it, and that I could manage to keep it up only by ceasing to look anywhere but within myself. Desolation everywhere and no way of eluding it except through a sort of selfishness that revolted me: "*I* at least . . ." or through what the Catholics call Faith, against which my reason protested. Was I therefore involved in all the suffering in the world?

I lacked dreadfully the cynicism it would have required to distract my mind. My temperament naturally led me toward joy, to be sure; but to maintain joy in me I should have had to be ignorant of or to forget too many things. The world was decidedly not ready to be able to get along without God; it was foundering in a dismal bankruptcy.

As for me, I take refuge in sympathy. It seems to me a realm that adversity cannot touch. I should like to make clear what I mean by this. I can do so only through some example. I must go back to a time when I had gone to meet the Roger Martin du Gard couple at the hotel at Hyères-Plage, not yet made untenable by the immediate proximity of a flying-field with its arrivals and departures at every hour of the day and night.[4] Complete understanding between us; I should have nothing but the best memories of it were it not for an inflammation of the ear that descended on me one night. It was after an evening when I had dragged my friends to the showing of a film that had delighted me and that I wanted them to see. Buster Keaton was won-

---

[4] This probably took place in the spring of 1925. In his *Journals* for 15 December 1946, Gide refers as he does here to "that night at Hyères-Plage."

derful in *The Laws of Hospitality*. We had got back from Hyères without mishap. But I was no sooner alone in my hotel room than the pain had begun. It soon became so violent that, driven from my bed, I was pacing up and down my room, not knowing what to do and wondering how I could bear it. Eventually, I could resist no longer; it seemed to me that only the sympathy I mentioned earlier could bring me some relief. My friends' rooms were separate and not very far from mine. Despite the hour (it was around two a.m.), I went and knocked on Roger's door: "I can't put up with it any longer; and you can't do anything about it . . . except to stretch out your hand and hold my hand in yours a little while. Just feeling your sympathy will relieve me, I'm sure." And so it was. However acute the pain, the friendly relief brought by Roger that night is the only thing I remember. What he was for me on that occasion is just what I should like to be for others. We can help one another so little, and often, alas, in such a ridiculously inadequate and awkward way. . . . But as soon as suffering is shared, it becomes easier to endure. Often the most painful thing is that it encounters the indifference of others. Having said this, let me add that there are many sufferings I claim to be imaginary and I am pitiless toward them: few things interest me less than so-called broken hearts and sentimental affairs. Often mockery suffices to cauterize them; it is soon evident that they involve a large share of self-pity, falsehood, and pretense. One is less really in love than one fancies, and it's a pity. Whereas the man dying of hunger and seeing his children die of hunger—these are real sufferings. And I take care, it goes without saying, not to shrug my shoulders in the face of those dilemmas, so frequent today, in which man is led to endure the worst sufferings in order to protect his dignity. They are the ones, above all, which elicit my sympathy, but a sympathy that most often is not in a position to express itself, especially as those are imponderable, secret, incalculable sufferings, but in which the very value of man is at stake. The lamentable thing is that his listed value has fallen so low today that it often merely makes people smile. It is essential to raise it. Let us be among those who try to do so.

Francis Jammes wrote a line long ago that made quite a hit:

The Vignys nauseate me with their dignity.[5]

---

[5] *Les Vigny m'emmerdent avec leur dignité.*

I can see how annoying such a constant concern for decorum can eventually become. It pays excessive attention to the opinion of others. I like a certain free-and-easy manner and yielding to one's nature; it is one of the forms of sincerity without which I don't feel at ease. There are many people who, on getting out of bed in the morning, spring to attention and try to live up to their official position. Even when alone, they take poses. Needless to say, what I mean is not that dignity, but rather a sort of respect for oneself and others that has no need to show externally.

As for what is called conceit, I fear that I have but a very small stock of it.

I recall that delightful drive home with François Mauriac. He was bringing me back from Malagar, where I had just spent with father and son one of the happiest weeks I can remember. Claude was driving. For the noon meal we stopped for some time at Brantôme. The innkeeper kept bowing before the Academician, who eventually became embarrassed at being the object of all the establishment's bowing and scraping. He took the innkeeper aside and tried to intimate to him that I too deserved some attentions. All this in a playful, bantering way with a charming sense of humor and of the proprieties. Thereupon the innkeeper, not quite catching my name, takes me for Mr. Gibbs, the maker of famous razor blades indiscreetly extolled on all the walls of the little town. At once the autograph book is brought. The Academician steps out of the limelight and all the attention goes to me.[6] This belongs to the special chapter on the misunderstandings of fame. For instance, I have sometimes been praised for remarks I never made or else made without any special intention. Let me cite this one which strikes me as rather funny so that I am careful not to disown it (although if I really said it, I did so spontaneously without the intentional germ of perfidy that gives it flavor). It took place after a private showing of a new film inspired by a cruel Strindberg play, *The Dance of Death*. Stroheim was excellent in it. As we came out, someone asked my opinion: "Did it interest you?" I answer simply: "At length." And this remark immediately goes from person to person.

Generally, the apocryphal wins out over reality, just as "bad money drives out good." Many an example could be cited; but, to stick to my own

---

[6] In his *Conversations with André Gide* (1951), based on his diary, Claude Mauriac reports even more amusingly this incident at Brantôme, which took place on 11 July 1939.

case, why shouldn't I take advantage of the opportunity to protest about this? Following the sensational break which caused us to reject Montfort's aid and that of his friends in the founding of the *Nouvelle Revue Française,* he went back to the editorship of *Les Marges,* which he strove to set up against us.[7] Some researcher, later on, will have fun picking out all the gibes aimed at us. They could be collected likewise in some newspaper or other (*L'Intransigeant,* I think). They are so cheap that I am ashamed to mention them. I shall let you be the judge. To his amazement, someone sees me turn toward a beggar in the street, hand him a fifty-centime coin, and hears me say to him (without my being aware, of course): "Yes, but when will you give it back?" It's even more stupid than nasty. But what of this anecdote! Born somewhere or other, it took on substance until it became an

---

[7] Eugène Montfort (1877–1936) had edited and completely written the periodical *Les Marges* from 1903 until 1908, when Gide and Schlumberger added him and his naturalistic aesthetic to the group that founded the *Nouvelle Revue Française.* With the appearance of the first issue in November 1908, all but Montfort were shocked by two articles written by friends of his. After painful explanations, Montfort left the group, which calmly produced a second No. 1. in February 1909 under the simple title suggested by Montfort which was to become famous in modern letters.

established fact: I invite a Russian Prince (others say a Spanish Prince) to an elaborate luncheon. As the meal approaches its end, my embarrassment becomes more and more obvious; it comes time to pay the bill, and I can't make up my mind to do so. Suddenly I get up and, making an effort, say to my guest: I am letting you pay, for I must confess that I am miserly. And I go. Basically I should not mind having the nerve to act that way at the expense of the "Prince." If, as others tell the story, he is a poor poet, it all becomes a rather nasty bit of caddishness. However that may be, there is not an atom of truth in the anecdote. It goes back, as I have said, to the time of the quarrel with Montfort. Now, when I see in the Milan newspaper *Corriere della Sera* for 13 January an Italian journalist named Indro Montanelli twice attribute the same silly remark to me in a visit he made to me recently, he will not be surprised if I consider that he lacks imagination.

There is what you are and what you would like to be, what you strive to seem. The greater the distance between the two, the more risky the game is. The funny thing is that the natural always rises to the surface despite the effort one makes to disguise it: certain exclamations and certain gestures escape you to reveal the spontaneous, and at once all the rest appears play-acting. Yet it would be so simple not to try to mask anything. This is why I should like the remark "I am miserly" if it were really an admission; but I have already explained myself on that point.[8] It can lead to misunderstandings. As for my sexual tastes, I have never hidden them except when they might embarrass others. Without exactly flaunting them, I have let them be apparent. This is partly because I have never thought they were such as to dishonor me. It is the free-and-easy, self-indulgent yielding to those tastes that dishonors; but this concerns me alone. Finally, there is the harm done to others, which must be calculated separately; and, in examining one of these cases, I should like to see a judge devoid of any prejudice dictated by other considerations than those provided by reason alone or, if you

---

[8] Gide frequently answered accusations of avarice, and probably the best statement he made on this subject appeared in his *Journals* for April 1929: "Close and niggardly . . . yes, I know that I am; and I admit that I am to excess. But this is because I prefer with all my heart being able to give what they who call me a miser are so willing to spend on themselves."

wish, social concern. But this is probably asking too much: opinion does not wait for such considerations; generally it is made up in advance.

I am going to risk a most unusual confession, which I can sum up in a few words: I have never (so far as I can remember) *panted* after anyone. This calls for explanation. Throughout my long life I have seen many people in love with a certain person of either sex, the mere sight of whom suggested: this can only end up in drama, for there is nothing to be expected or hoped for; no reciprocity is possible. In my case this is enough to inhibit all desire in me; an instinct warns me at once, and this is one of the secrets of my happiness. When I feel in advance that I shall be unable to stir someone physically, he ceases at once to stir me. Oh! how I pity anyone burning with love who consumes himself in vain! But one doesn't order one's desires. Mine unfailingly respond to some appetite on the part of the other person, which I foresee, and even without any provocation. As a result of experience, my flair in this regard has become almost infallible. I must add that such appetite is much more frequent than I used to suppose, so that I have known but few rebuffs; and the total inhibition of my desires in the other cases is so rapid that there could be no question, strictly speaking, of disappointments. Relations were in no way modified by this. Let me add this too: the moral or intellectual or sentimental realm in me is separate from erotic excitation to the point that one excludes the other, and that my many friendships have always been utterly free of any sensual intrusion. Doubtless it is not useless to state this, for some have occasionally made serious mistakes about this. Without any resolve, without any effort, my friendships have been appropriately chaste—whence their solidity and duration. I take no pleasure in writing these last few lines, but people's imagination goes so far astray in this regard that I think I must insist.

The great number of confidences I have been in a position to receive has convinced me that the variety of cases of homosexuality is much greater than that of cases of heterosexuality. And, furthermore, the irrepressible loathing a homosexual may feel for another whose appetites are not the same as his is something of which the heterosexual has no idea; he lumps them all together so as to be able to throw them all overboard at one and the same time, and this is obviously much more expedient. I tried in so far as I could to make the distinction between pederasts in the Greek sense of the word (love of boys) and inverts, but no one deigned to see anything in this but a rather footless discrimination, and I had to give up. It's probably better not to try again, but rather to note down a peculiarity of my nature: my desire, made up in part of curiosity, flags very rapidly, and even, most often, when pleasure is at its best, I feel satisfied at the first contact. I feel no need of resumptions or repetitions. So that the other is disappointed. It is very rare that, in any mating whatever, one of the two does not remain, more or less painfully, unsatisfied.

I have never said so much on this subject; but it seems that the more is said about this matter the more there is to say. The hard thing is to stop.

However that may be, I have strayed considerably from what I first wanted to say, though it is much simpler: the number of those who are destined to cut a figure in the world and who are willing, who manage to remain natural, who are not concerned with the opinion that the gallery (were it made up of but one person) will have of them, is extremely limited: one strikes a pose, puffs out one's chest, raises one's voice. Even for the sake of no one but Friday, Robinson Crusoe has a tendency to pose; the workman for the sake of the boss; the boss for the sake of the workman. Yes, a completely natural manner is such a rare thing that it may well look like affectation. And perhaps it is natural, after all, that each individual should talk and act in terms of others. The little effort of re-establishing the truth (as in the theater) is not without interest, and belongs to the pleasure we get from the drama. Nevertheless, La Bruyère was right (as has already been pointed out): there is no occasion for Tartuffe to say, except on the stage: "Laurent, put away my hair shirt and my scourge." Such exaggeration is worth while only on the stage . . . and even then . . ."[9]

Now, the question arises. It constantly rises before me: What will remain of all this? Oh, I am not speaking particularly of what I have just written, which could be effaced with one stroke of the pen, but of all that is being written today, in France and elsewhere. What will remain of our culture, of

---

[9] In his portrait of the true hypocrite Onuphre in the *Caractères*, La Bruyère criticizes Molière's Tartuffe for being too obviously insincere. The accomplished hypocrite, he claims, would make people assume that he wore a hair shirt and scourged himself without ever mentioning such things.

France itself, of what we have lived for? . . . Let's make up our minds that everything is destined to disappear.

And here are the last lines, written on 13 February 1951, six days before death:

No, I cannot assert that with the end of this notebook all will be finished; that all will be over. Perhaps I shall have a desire to add something. To add something or other. To make an addition. Perhaps. At the last moment, to add something still . . . I am sleepy, to be sure. But I don't feel like sleeping. It strikes me that I could be even more tired. It is I don't know what hour of the night or of the morning. . . . Do I still have something to say? Still something or other to say?

My own position in the sky, in relation to the sun, must not make me consider the dawn any less beautiful.[1]

~~~~~~~~~~

[1] In the margin Gide added: "This page has no connection with the preceding ones."

Then lower on the page: "The too neutral grayish blue of Catherine's coat was miraculously balanced, subsequently, by the unexpected addition of her toque. The whole thing exquisitely tasteful, of course."

INDEX

i

INDEX

INDEX

A NOTE ON THE AUTHOR

André Gide was born in Paris in 1869 and died there in 1951. Besides his *Journals* (1939, 1944, 1950), his major works include *The Immoralist* (1902), *The Counterfeiters* (1926), *Strait Is the Gate* (1909), and *Lafcadio's Adventures* (1914). He also wrote plays, essays, short stories, and books of travel. Gide was awarded the Nobel Prize for Literature in 1947.